THE COMPLETE BOOK OF

VEGETARIAN COOKING

THE COMPLETE BOOK OF
VEGETARIAN COOKING

Edited by
Veronica Sperling & Christine McFadden

First published in Great Britain in 1996 by
Parragon Book Service Ltd
Unit 13–17
Avonbridge Trading Estate
Atlantic Road
Avonmouth
Bristol BS11 9QD

ISBN: 0-75252-059-8

Printed in Italy

Produced by Haldane Mason, London

Acknowledgements
Art Direction: Ron Samuels
Design: Digital Artworks Partnership Ltd

Material contained in this book has previously appeared in
Vegetarian Main Meals and *Low-Fat Cooking* by Kathryn Hawkins
Vegetarian Dinner Parties, *Vegetarian Barbecues*
and *Cooking on a Budget* by Sue Ashworth
Recipes with Yogurt by Pamela Westland
Quick & Easy Meals by Carole Handslip
Soups & Broths and *Cooking for One or Two* by Rosemary Wadey
Vegetarian Thai Cooking, Barbecues and
Puddings & Desserts by Cara Hobday

Contents

VEGETARIAN CUISINE

People choose to eat vegetarian food for all sorts of different reasons, whether on moral grounds, for health reasons, for economy or simply because they prefer the flavour. Whatever the motive, one thing is certain - everyone enjoys good food, and vegetarian food can be as good as, and indeed often better than, traditional meat and fish dishes. Vegetarian meals are perfect for entertaining or just for the family to enjoy, and can be easily adapted to suit all tastes.

VEGETARIAN NUTRITION

Vegetarian food is extremely healthy, and provides all the important vitamins, minerals, proteins, carbohydrates and fats that make up a nutritious, well-balanced diet. And because you tend to eat more fruit, vegetables, grains and pulses (legumes), the diet is rich in complex carbohydrates, your primary source of energy and fibre, which helps to keep your body vibrant and healthy.

Protein

Obtaining sufficient protein is not a problem in a vegetarian diet – there are plenty of foods from which to choose. Eggs, cheese, milk, nuts and beans, soya products such as TVP (texturized vegetable protein) soya milk and tofu (bean curd), Quorn or mycoprotein are all excellent sources. Make sure that you eat a wide variety of these foods to get the full range of protein that your body needs.

Fat

Another additional benefit of following a vegetarian diet is that it can be quite low in fat. The main sources of fat in your diet will be from vegetable, nut and olive oils, dairy foods, nuts and any products containing these ingredients. So slimmers can succeed in losing weight following a vegetarian diet, provided they keep an eye on their overall fat intake.

Carbohydrates

A vegetarian diet is rich in complex carbohydrates, found in starchy foods such as brown rice, oats, and whole-wheat pasta and bread. These are particularly useful to dieters, as they ensure a steady release of energy and a stable blood sugar level.

Vitamins

Fruit and vegetables are packed with important vitamins, essential for our general well-being and the healthy functioning of our bodies. If you follow a vegetarian diet, you can't go far wrong.

The best sources of vitamin A are yellow fruits and vegetables and some green vegetables – apricots, peaches, spinach and carrots, for example. It is also present in butter and added to margarines. Vitamin A helps us to resist infections and keeps the skin, hair, eyes and body tissues healthy.

The B group vitamins act as a catalyst in the releasing of energy from food. They are also vital for the maintenance of a healthy nervous system and red blood cells. Apart from vitamin B12, all the B vitamins can be found in yeast and whole-

grain cereals, especially wheat flour and wheatgerm. Vegetarians eating a wide variety of foods should therefore have no problem in obtaining enough B vitamins, although vegans (who do not eat dairy products) need to include some sort of B12 supplement in their diet.

Vitamin C is well known for helping to prevent infections and is firmly believed by many to assist in warding off, as well as curing, winter colds and 'flu. Eat foods rich in vitamin C with iron-rich foods, as it helps to increase the uptake of iron. Fresh fruit, leafy vegetables, tomatoes, (bell) peppers and potatoes are all good sources. Avoid drinking tea, coffee and certain soft drinks with foods that contain vitamin C, as the caffeine can decrease the amount of vitamin C your body subsequently absorbs. Since vitamin C is easily destroyed during cooking, take care when boiling vegetables to use a small amount of water and to cook them as quickly as possible. This will minimize the risk of the vitamin leaching into the cooking water.

The other important vitamin for good health is vitamin D, which enables the body to absorb calcium, thus providing strong bones and teeth. Vitamin D is often known as the 'sunshine vitamin', as the body can manufacture its own supply from exposure to sunlight. Good food sources include eggs, cheese, margarine and butter.

Minerals

Minerals are another group of vital nutrients that are needed by the human body. Although only minute amounts are required, minerals need to be supplied on a regular basis. It makes sense to get to know which foods contain them, and make sure you are getting plenty of these in your diet. There should be no problem as long as you eat a wide variety of foods.

Calcium is found in milk, cheese, yogurt and other dairy products, leafy green vegetables, bread, nuts, seeds and dried fruits. Iron is found in beans, seeds, nuts, eggs, cocoa and chocolate, wholemeal (whole wheat) bread, leafy green vegetables and dried fruits (especially apricots and figs). Other important minerals include magnesium, phosphorus, potassium and zinc.

THE VEGETARIAN SHOPPING BASKET

When shopping for vegetarian foods, make sure that you are not buying animal products unawares. Choose cheese that is made from vegetarian rennet; buy agar-agar or gelozone instead of gelatine; select a vegetarian suet instead of beef suet – no, you won't have to forego delicious dumplings! Be aware of what you are spreading on your bread too. Some margarines are not suitable as they contain both fish oils and animal fats, so check that you are buying a brand made entirely of vegetable oil. Butter is perfect, unless you are a vegan.

THE VEGETARIAN STORE-CUPBOARD

A well-stocked store-cupboard forms the backbone of any good cook's kitchen, and it is always useful to have plenty of basic foods ready to hand. Use the following information as a checklist when you need to replenish your stocks.

Flours

You will need to keep a selection of flours: plain (all-purpose) and self-raising flour if you want to make your own bread, and wholemeal (whole wheat) flour, either for using on its own or for combining with white flour for cakes and pastries. You may also like to keep some rice flour and cornflour (cornstarch) for thickening sauces and to add to cakes, biscuits and puddings. Buckwheat, chick-pea (garbanzo bean) and soya flours can also be bought. These are useful for pancakes and for combining with other flours to add different flavours and textures.

Grains

A good variety of grains is essential. For rice, choose from long-grain, basmati, Italian arborio for making risotto, short-grain for puddings, wild rice to add interest. Look out for fragrant Thai rice, jasmine rice and combinations of different varieties to add colour and texture to your dishes. When choosing your rice, remember that brown rice is a better source of vitamin B1 and fibre.

Other grains add variety to the diet. Try to include some barley (whole grain or pearl), millet, bulgur wheat, polenta (made from maize), oats (oatmeal, oatflakes or oatbran), semolina – including cous-cous (from which it is made), sago and tapioca.

Pasta

Pasta has become much more popular recently, and there are many types and shapes to choose from. Keep a good selection, and always make sure you have the basic lasagne sheets, tagliatelle or fettuccine (flat ribbons) and spaghetti. Try spinach- or tomato-flavoured varieties for a change, and sample some of the many fresh pastas now available. Better still, make your own – handrolling pasta, while undoubtedly time-consuming, can be very satisfying, but you can buy a special machine for rolling the dough and cutting certain shapes. You could also buy a wooden 'pasta tree' on which to hang the pasta to dry, in which case you might find you get enthusiastic help especially if you have small children!

Pulses (legumes)

Pulses (legumes) are very important in a vegetarian diet as they are a valuable source of protein, vitamins and minerals. Stock up on soya beans, haricot (navy) beans, red kidney beans, cannellini beans, chick-peas (garbanzo beans), all types of lentils, split peas and butter beans. Buy dried pulses (legumes) for soaking and cooking yourself, or canned varieties for speed and convenience.

It is important to cook dried red and black kidney beans in plenty of vigorously boiling water for 15 minutes to destroy harmful toxins in the outer skin. Drain and rinse the beans, and then continue to simmer until the beans are tender. Soya beans should be boiled for 1 hour, as they contain a substance that inhibits protein absorption.

Spices and herbs

A good selection of spices and herbs is important for adding variety and interest to your cooking – add to your range each time you try a new recipe. There are some good spice mixtures available – try Cajun, Chinese five-spice, Indonesian piri-piri and the different curry blends. Try grinding your own spices with a mortar and pestle, or in a coffee mill, to make your own blends, or just experiment with those that you can buy. Although spices will keep well, don't leave them in the cupboard for too long, as they may lose some of their strength. Buy small amounts as you need them.

Fresh herbs are always preferable to dried, but it is essential to have dried ones in stock as a useful back-up. Keep the basics such as thyme, rosemary, bay leaves and some good Mediterranean mixtures for Italian and French cooking.

Chillies

These come both fresh and dried and in colours from green through yellow, orange and red to brown. The 'hotness' varies so use with caution, but as a guide the smaller they are the hotter they will be. The seeds are hottest and are usually discarded. When cutting chillies with bare hands do not touch your eyes; the juices will cause severe irritation.

Chilli powder should also be used sparingly. Check whether the powder is pure chilli or a chilli seasoning or blend, which should be milder. Chilli sauces are also used widely in oriental cookery, but again they vary in strength from hot to exceedingly hot, as well as in sweetness.

Nuts and seeds

As well as adding protein, vitamins and useful fats to the diet, nuts and seeds add important flavour and texture to vegetarian meals. To bring out the flavour of nuts and seeds, grill or roast them until lightly browned.

Make sure that you keep a good supply of almonds, brazils, cashews, chestnuts (dried or canned), hazelnuts, peanuts, pecans, pistachios, pine kernels (nuts) and walnuts. Coconut – either creamed or desiccated (shredded) – is useful too.

For your seed collection, have sesame, sunflower, pumpkin and poppy. Pumpkin seeds in particular are an excellent source of zinc.

Dried fruits

Currants, raisins, sultanas (golden raisins), dates, apples, apricots, figs, pears, peaches, prunes, paw-paws (papayas), mangoes, figs, bananas and pineapples can all be purchased dried and can be used in lots of different recipes. When buying dried fruits, look for untreated varieties: for example, buy figs that have not been rolled in sugar, and choose unsulphured apricots, if they are available.

Though dried fruits are a healthier alternative to biscuits (cookies) and sweets (candies), they are still high in calories, being a natural source of sugar.

Oils and fats

Oils are useful for adding subtle flavourings to foods, so it is a good idea to have a selection in your store-cupboard. Use a light olive oil for cooking and extra-virgin olive oil for salad dressings. Use sunflower oil as a good general-purpose oil and select one or two speciality oils to add character to different dishes. Sesame oil is wonderful in stir-fries; hazelnut and walnut oils are superb in salad dressings.

Oils and fats add flavour to foods, and contain the important fat-soluble vitamins A, D, E and K. Remember all fats and oils are high in calories, and that oils are higher in calories than butter or margarine - one tablespoon of oil contains 134 calories, whereas one tablespoon of butter or margarine contains 110 calories. When you are using oil in dressings or adding it to a wok or frying pan (skillet), it is a good idea to measure it - it's easy to use twice as much without realizing.

Vinegars

Choose three or four vinegars – red or white wine, cider, light malt, tarragon, sherry or balsamic vinegar, to name just a few. Each will add its own character to your recipes.

Mustards

Mustards are made from black, brown or white mustard seeds which are ground, mixed with spices and then, usually, mixed with vinegar.

Meaux mustard is made from mixed mustard seeds and has a grainy texture with a warm, spicy taste.

Dijon mustard, made from husked and ground mustard seeds, is medium-hot and has a sharp flavour. Its versatility in salads and with barbecues makes it an ideal mustard for the vegetarian. It is made in Dijon, France, and only mustard made there can be labelled as such.

German mustard is mild sweet/sour and is best used in Scandinavian and German dishes.

Bottled sauces

Soy sauce is widely used in all Eastern cookery and is made from fermented yellow soya beans mixed with wheat, salt, yeast and sugar. It comes in both light and dark varieties. Light soy sauce tends to be rather salty, whereas dark soy sauce tends to be sweeter and is more often used in dips and sauces.

Teriyaki sauce gives an authentic Japanese flavouring to stir-fries. Thick and dark brown, it contains soy sauce, vinegar, sesame oil and spices as main ingredients.

Black bean and yellow bean sauces add an instant authentic Chinese flavour to stir-fries. Black bean sauce is the stronger; the yellow bean variety is milder and is excellent with vegetables.

Useful extras

Tahini (sesame seed paste), yeast extract, sea salt, black and green peppercorns, tomato and garlic purées (pastes), vegetable stock (bouillon) cubes, dried yeast, gelozone or agar-agar are all useful store-cupboard additions.

THE VEGETARIAN FRIDGE AND FREEZER

Thankfully, food manufacturers have wised up to the fact that lots of us love to eat vegetarian food, so it is now possible to choose from a huge range of prepared meals from the chilled or frozen food cabinets. These are excellent standbys for when you want a meal in a hurry, and they add variety and choice to the diet. Pasta dishes, vegetable bakes and burgers, curries, flans and quiches are just some of the dishes to choose from.

Besides stocking a selection of ready-made meals, freeze other basics such as frozen pastries (shortcrust, filo or puff pastry); a selection of breads, such as pitta, French bread, rolls or part-baked bread; pre-cooked pasta dishes, pasta sauces, stocks, breadcrumbs, home-made soups and sauces, flan cases, pancakes, pizza bases, and so on. All these will be useful when you are short of time.

THE SECRET OF SUCCESS

As with any cooking, the choice of ingredients is of paramount importance. If they are fresh and of good quality, you are well on your way to achieving delicious food. Not only will the flavours be better, but so will the colours, textures and nutritive value. Fresh fruit and vegetables lose their vitamin content very quickly if stored for too long, so buy from the freshest possible source, and use soon after buying.

BASIC RECIPES

Vegetarian stocks and sauces are invaluable for many recipes. Here are a few basics.

Fresh Vegetable Stock

This can be kept chilled for up to three days or frozen for up to three months. Salt is not added when cooking the stock: it is better to season it according to the dish in which it is to be used. Makes 1.5 litres/2½ pints/6¼ cups.

250 g/8 oz shallots
1 large carrot, diced
1 celery stalk, chopped
½ fennel bulb
1 garlic clove
1 bay leaf
a few fresh parsley and tarragon sprigs
2 litres/3½ pints/8¾ cups water
pepper

Put all the ingredients in a large saucepan and bring to the boil. Skim off the surface scum with a flat spoon and reduce to a gentle simmer. Partially cover and cook for 45 minutes. Leave to cool.

Line a sieve (strainer) with clean muslin (cheesecloth) and put over a large jug or bowl. Pour the stock through the sieve (strainer). Discard the herbs and vegetables. Cover and store in small quantities in the refrigerator for up to three days.

Tahini Cream

Tahini is a paste made from sesame seeds. This nutty-flavoured sauce is good served with Kofta Kebabs (page 142) and other Middle Eastern dishes such as falafel. Makes 150 ml/¼ pt/⅔ cup.

3 tbsp tahini
6 tbsp water
2 tsp lemon juice
1 garlic clove, crushed
salt and pepper

Blend together the tahini and water. Stir in the lemon juice and garlic. Season with salt and freshly ground black pepper.

Béchamel Sauce

This basic white sauce can be used in all kinds of dishes. Flavour it with grated cheese or chopped fresh herbs if you like. Makes 600 ml/1 pint/2½ cups.

600 ml/1 pint/2½ cups milk
4 cloves
1 bay leaf
pinch of freshly grated nutmeg
30 g/1 oz/2 tbsp butter or margarine
30 g/1 oz/¼ cup plain (all-purpose) flour
salt and pepper

Put the milk in a saucepan and add the cloves, bay leaf and nutmeg. Gradually bring to the boil. Remove from the heat and leave for 15 minutes.

Melt the butter or margarine in another saucepan and stir in the flour to form a roux. Cook, stirring, for 1 minute.

Remove from the heat. Strain the milk and gradually blend into the roux.

Return to the heat and bring to the boil, stirring, until the sauce thickens. Season and add any flavourings.

SALADS

*Salads are such a versatile way of eating, and the variety of ingredients
is so great, that they can be made to suit any occasion, from a light piquant
starter to a more substantial dish to serve as a main course, or a mixture
of exotic fruits for a delicious dessert.*

SALAD INGREDIENTS

A salad is the ideal emergency meal. It is quick to 'rustle up' and there are times when you might discover that you already have a really good combination of ingredients to hand when you need to present a meal-in-a-moment. A splash of culinary inspiration, and you will find you have prepared a fantastic salad that you had no idea was lurking in your kitchen.

Salads can be fruity, eggy, cheesy, made with grains or pulses (legumes), or just fresh green – all are highly nutritious. They are also generally low in calories if you go easy on the dressing, or use a fat-free dressing. It is easy to make a salad look attractive and appetizing, thus encouraging your family to eat fruit and vegetables. It is also often a welcome dish to serve alongside richer offerings.

Supermarkets now stock many unusual ingredients, which can add interest to an ordinary salad. Experiment with new fruits and vegetables, buying them in small quantities to lend unusual flavours to salads made from cheaper ingredients. Make sure you always use the freshest ingredients to ensure a successful salad. Try to ensure that you buy fruit and vegetables at their peak and use them within a few days of buying.

Herbs

Every salad can be turned into something special with the addition of a few carefully chosen herbs to add flavour and a delicious aroma. The recipes in this book make liberal use of fresh herbs, adding a unique 'zip' to the food. Experiment with different varieties each time you make a salad or a dressing; try marjoram, thyme, chives, basil, mint, fennel and dill as well as the ubiquitous parsley. Basil goes especially well with tomatoes, and fennel or dill are particularly good with cucumber or beetroot salads.

Flowers

For an extra-special salad, add a few edible flowers, which look particularly colourful and attractive especially when mixed with a variety of salad leaves (greens). Common sense is the best guide as to which flowers may be used whole and which should have the petals gently separated from the calyx. Borage, primroses, violas, pot marigolds, nasturtiums, violets, rock geraniums and rose petals are all suitable, imparting a sweetness and intense colour contrast to any green salad. Chive flowers have a good strong flavour – the pretty mauve flower heads should be separated into florets before sprinkling over the salad.

It is, of course, important that the flowers should look fresh and clean. If they need washing, be sure to handle with great care. Gently pat dry with paper towels and store them in a rigid polythene container in the refrigerator until required.

It goes without saying that flowers which have been sprayed with insecticide should not be used.

Nuts

In addition to colour and flavour, salads need texture, which can be achieved by combining crunchy ingredients with softer fruits and vegetables. Nuts are particularly useful in this respect, contributing a pleasant crunchiness as well as flavour. Many nuts taste even better if they are browned before use. These include almonds, hazelnuts, pine kernels (nuts) and peanuts. To brown nuts, put them on a baking sheet and place in a hot oven for 5–10 minutes until golden brown. Pine kernels (nuts) may also be browned by placing in a dry heavy-based frying pan (skillet) and shaking over a high heat until golden.

Salad leaves (greens)

Supermarkets now stock a wonderful variety of previously-hard-to-find salad leaves (greens), so experiment with different types. The raw leaves from young leafy vegetables can also be used.

CHICORY (ENDIVE) This is available from autumn (fall) to spring and, with its slightly bitter flavour, makes an interesting addition to winter salads. Choose firm, tightly packed cones with yellow leaf tips. Avoid any with damaged leaves or leaf tips that are turning green as they will be rather too bitter. Red chicory (endive) is also available.

CHINESE LEAVES These are a most useful salad ingredient available in the autumn (fall) and winter months. Shred them fairly finely and use them as a base, adding bean-shoots and peppery leaves such as watercress or dandelion.

COS (ROMAINE) **LETTUCE** This is a superb variety used especially in Caesar salad. It has long, narrow, bright green leaves with a wonderfully crisp texture.

ENDIVE (CHICORY) A slightly bitter-tasting but attractive curly-leaved salad plant. There are two varieties: the curly endive (frisée) which has a mop head of light green frilly leaves and the Batavia endive (escarole) which has broader, smoother leaves. Before they mature, both varieties have their leaves tied together to blanch the centres, which produces tender, succulent leaves.

FEUILLE DE CHÊNE (OAK LEAF) This red-tinged, delicately flavoured lettuce is good when mixed with other leaves, both for the contrast in flavour and the contrast in colour.

ICEBERG LETTUCE This has pale green, densely packed leaves. It may appear expensive, but is in fact extremely good value when compared with other lettuces by weight. It has a fresh, crisp texture and keeps well in the refrigerator.

LAMB'S LETTUCE (CORN SALAD) This is so called because its dark green leaves resemble a lamb's tongue. It is also known as corn salad and the French call it mâche. It is well worth looking out for when it is in season both for its flavour and its appearance.

PURSLANE This has fleshy stalks and rosettes of succulent green leaves which have a sharp, clean flavour.

RADICCHIO This is a variety of chicory (endive) originating in Italy. It looks rather like a small, tightly packed red lettuce. It is quite expensive but comparatively few leaves are needed, as it has a bitter flavour. The leaves are a deep purple with a white contrasting rib. They add character to any green salad.

ROCKET (ARUGULA, ROQUETTE) The young green leaves of this plant have a distinctive warm peppery flavour and are delicious in green salads.

ROUND OR CABBAGE LETTUCE This is the one most familiar

to us all. Try to avoid the hothouse variety as the leaves are limp and floppy.

WATERCRESS This has a fresh peppery taste which makes it a welcome addition to many salads. It is available throughout the year, though it is less good when flowering, or early in the season when the leaves are small.

Preparing salad leaves (greens)

Whichever salad leaves (greens) you choose, they should be firm and crisp with no sign of browning or wilting. They should be handled with care because salad leaves (greens) bruise easily.

To prepare, pull off and discard all damaged outer leaves and wash the remaining leaves in cold salted water to remove any insects, then dry them thoroughly. This can be done either by patting the leaves dry with paper towels, spinning them in a salad spinner, or by placing them in a clean tea towel (dish cloth), gathering up the loose ends and swinging the tea towel (dish cloth) around vigorously.

Dress the salad leaves (greens) just before serving. If you dress it any earlier the leaves will wilt.

Dressings

All salads depend on being well dressed and so it is necessary to use the best ingredients. The principal ingredients in a salad dressing are oil and vinegar, with a variety of other flavourings that can be varied to suit the particular salad.

The choice of oil is particularly important. Oils are produced from various nuts, seeds and beans and each has its own flavour. Unrefined oils, although more expensive, are worth using for their superior taste.

OLIVE OIL is the best oil for most salad dressings. Choose the green-tinged, fruity oil labelled 'extra virgin' or 'first pressing'. It has a distinctive taste and aroma.

SESAME OIL has a strong nutty tang and is particularly good with oriental-type salads.

SUNFLOWER AND SAFFLOWER OIL are neutral-flavoured oils and can be mixed with olive oil or used alone to produce a lighter dressing. Mayonnaise made with a combination of one of these oils and olive oil has a lighter consistency than one made from olive oil only.

WALNUT AND HAZELNUT OIL have the most wonderful flavour and aroma, and are usually mixed with olive oil in a French dressing. They are well worth their higher price and are especially good with slightly bitter salad plants such as chicory (endive), radicchio or spinach.

A good dressing needs a touch of acidity. Good quality vinegars such as wine, cider, sherry or herb-flavoured vinegars are ideal, but malt vinegar is far too harsh and overpowers the subtle balance of the dressing. Lemon juice may be used and is often preferable if the salad is fruit-based.

CIDER VINEGAR is reputed to contain many healthy properties and valuable nutrients. It has a light, subtle flavour redolent of the fruit from which it is made.

WINE VINEGAR is the one most commonly used for French dressing; either red or white will do.

SHERRY VINEGAR has a rich mellow flavour which blends well with walnut and hazelnut oils, but is equally good by itself.

BALSAMIC VINEGAR is dark and mellow with a sweet/sour flavour. It is expensive but you need only a few drops or at most a teaspoonful to give a wonderful taste. It is made in the area around Modena in Italy.

FLAVOURED VINEGARS can be made from cider and wine vinegar. To do this, steep your chosen ingredient in a small bottle of vinegar for anything up to two weeks.
Particularly good additions are basil, tarragon, garlic, thyme, mint or rosemary. Raspberry wine vinegar can be made by adding about twelve raspberries to a bottle of vinegar.

SALAD DRESSINGS

Make up a large bottle of your favourite dressing. Here are some recipes for you to try:

Sesame Dressing

A piquant dressing with a rich creamy texture.

2 tbsp sesame paste (tahini)
2 tbsp cider vinegar
2 tbsp medium sherry
2 tbsp sesame oil
1 tbsp soy sauce
1 garlic clove, crushed

Put the sesame paste (tahini) in a bowl and gradually mix in the vinegar and sherry until smooth. Add the remaining ingredients and mix together thoroughly.

Tomato Dressing

This completely fat-free dressing is ideal if you are counting calories.

120 ml/4 fl oz/½ cup tomato juice
1 garlic clove, crushed
2 tbsp lemon juice
1 tbsp soy sauce
1 tsp clear honey
2 tbsp chopped chives
salt and pepper

Put all the ingredients into a screw-top jar and shake vigorously until well mixed.

Apple & Cider Vinegar Dressing

2 tbsp sunflower oil
2 tbsp concentrated apple juice
2 tbsp cider vinegar
1 tbsp Meaux mustard
1 garlic clove, crushed
salt and pepper

Put all the ingredients together in a screw-top jar and shake vigorously.

Green Herb Dressing

A pale green dressing with a fresh flavour, ideal with cauliflower or broccoli.

15 g/½ oz/¼ cup parsley
15 g/½ oz/¼ cup mint
15 g/½ oz/¼ cup chives
1 garlic clove, crushed
150 ml/¼ pint/⅔ cup natural yogurt
salt and pepper

Remove the stalks from the parsley and mint and put the leaves in a blender or food processor with the chives, garlic and yogurt. Add seasoning to taste. Blend until smooth, then store in refrigerator until needed.

WOK COOKERY

Wok cookery is an excellent technique for vegetarians as it enables you to serve up delicious dishes of crisp, tasty vegetables in minutes.

Preparing food for the wok

Always read the whole recipe before you start. Make sure everything is prepared and all ingredients are to hand before you actually start to cook, otherwise the first ingredients will be overcooked before the others are ready to add.

Although oriental cooks tend to use a variety of cleavers for chopping, a good sharp kitchen knife will do just as well. All ingredients should be cut into uniform sizes and shapes with as many cut surfaces exposed as possible, hence the practice of cutting on the slant or diagonal, or into julienne strips or matchsticks.

Stir-frying

This is the most popular method of cooking in a wok. Once the food has been prepared and you are ready to begin, add the oil to the wok and heat it, swirling it round until it is really hot. If it is sufficiently hot the ingredients added should sizzle and begin to cook.

Most recipes begin by cooking the onions, garlic and ginger, because they flavour the oil. The heat may need to be lowered a little at first but must be increased again as the other ingredients are added. Gas probably gives the best results because of the speed of controlling the heat, and the fact that the curved base of the wok fits so well into the hob. Electric and solid fuel hobs are more efficient if you are using a flat-bottomed wok.

Always add the ingredients in the order they are listed in the recipe. While the food is cooking, keep stirring. When you add a sauce or liquid at the end of a recipe, first push the cooked food to the side of the wok so the sauce heats as quickly as possible, then toss the food back into the sauce over a high heat so that it boils rapidly and thickens the sauce. Once the food is cooked, serve it as soon as possible.

Deep-frying

A wok is usually used for frying battered egg-and-crumbed morsels of food or food encased in pastry. The best oil to use is groundnut, which has a high smoke point and mild flavour, so it will neither burn nor impart taste to the food.

If you have a round-bottomed wok, use a metal wok stand to keep it stable during cooking. It is not necessary to preheat the wok. Simply add the oil (about 600 ml/1 pint/2 ½ cups should be sufficient) and heat until the required temperature is reached; use a thermometer or test until a cube of bread takes 30 seconds to brown.

The cooking time is determined by the size of the ingredients to be cooked, and it is essential that the oil is hot enough to seal the batter or pastry as quickly as possible without the food absorbing any more oil than necessary. When golden brown, remove with a slotted spoon and drain on paper towels. Serve at once to retain the food's crispness.

Steaming

To steam food you need a large wok and a bamboo steamer with a lid. The wok needs a little water in the bottom but it must not reach the base of the bamboo steamer when it is in position: stand the steamer on a trivet. The steamer has several layers, which can be stacked on top of each other. This means more than one type of food can be cooked at the same time. Put the food on a plate that will just fit into the steamer and place it carefully in one of the layers. Add seasoning, herbs and flavourings, then put on the lid and steam until tender. Make sure the wok does not boil dry by adding extra water when necessary.

If you don't have a bamboo steamer, you can still steam food in the wok. Simply put a plate on a metal or wooden trivet in the wok with water to just below the plate and cover with a lid.

Braising/simmering

The wok can also be used as a saucepan and is excellent for making stir-fry soups, for example. Just stir-fry the ingredients in a little oil, add the liquid seasonings and simmer either uncovered or with a lid. With this type of soup the vegetables should still have a good 'bite' to them, so the cooking time is a lot less than that of traditional soups.

Pan-frying and braising are speeded up using a wok because of the improved heat distribution. Simply fry the ingredients quickly, then add the stock or sauce, cover and simmer gently until tender. Sometimes it is better not to cover the wok so that the cooking liquid is reduced, intensifying the flavours even more. Whichever method is used, stir occasionally to prevent any possibility of sticking.

VEGETARIAN BARBECUES

There are so many tasty and nutritious vegetarian dishes that can be cooked over hot coals – after all, barbecuing is just an alternative method of cooking by direct heat.

Planning your barbecue

Whenever food is being barbecued, there always seems to be a long wait, so have a few dips and nibbles to keep your hungry guests satisfied. These can all be made in advance and kept chilled until needed. Raw vegetable crudités can be prepared beforehand, too.

Barbecues always take longer to get going than you expect, so allow plenty of time. Don't be tempted to start cooking too soon, or the coals will not be ready. The flames should have died down and the coals reduced to a steady glow before you begin.

Don't attempt to cook for a large party on a small barbecue, as it could take hours to feed everyone! In this situation, it is better to cook most of the food in the kitchen, and either provide only a few barbecued items, or use the barbecue to finish part-cooked foods. Vegetarian sausages and burgers are ideal, as they cook quickly and can be barbecued in large quantities even on a small barbecue.

Advance preparations

Many foods for barbecuing will benefit from being marinated, especially dishes using tofu (bean curd) or Quorn (mycopro-tein), which absorb the flavour of the marinade. You can buy tofu (bean curd) in four varieties – smoked, firm, soft or silken; use smoked or firm for kebabs, soft for adding to burgers and silken for adding to sauces and dips.

Have your kebabs ready-threaded for quick cooking; if possible, choose flat metal skewers so that the food does not slide as the kebabs are turned. Alternatively, use bamboo sticks – but remember to soak these in water beforehand so that they do not burn over the hot coals and ruin the food.

Make sweet and savoury sauces in advance if you can, ready to be brought out at the last moment.

Cooking tips

First and foremost, treat food for barbecuing with care – it should be kept chilled in the refrigerator or in a cool box, complete with ice packs, until ready to cook.

Light the barbecue in plenty of time, remembering that you will need about 45 minutes for charcoal to heat and about 10–15 minutes for a gas barbecue to become hot enough. Food cooks best over glowing embers, not smoking fuel, so avoid putting the food over the hot coals until the smoking has subsided.

Oil the barbecue rack lightly before adding the food, to help to prevent it from sticking, and oil the skewers, tongs and barbecue fork for the same reason.

Have some fresh herbs to hand for throwing on to the coals. They smell wonderful as they burn, and will add extra flavour to your food. Woody herbs burn slowly, so they are good choices.

Control the heat by adjusting the distance of the food from the coals, or by altering the controls on a gas barbecue. Ideally, food should not be cooked too quickly, or else it will blacken and char on the outside before the middle is cooked – it needs time for the distinctive barbecued taste to be imparted.

Cooking vegetables

For kebabs, choose a mixture of vegetables that will all cook at the same rate, and cut the chunks into roughly the same size. Choose from aubergines (eggplants), tomatoes, sliced corn-on-the-cob or baby sweetcorn, mushrooms and courgettes (zucchini). New pota-toes, onions, carrots, parsnips and Jerusalem artichokes can also be barbecued, but will need pre-cooking first.

If you are going to serve jacket potatoes, cook them first too – either conventionally or in a microwave oven. Wrap in foil and keep warm to one side of the barbecue, ready for filling. Alternatively, you can finish cooking potatoes directly on the grid over the coals, barbecuing them until the skins are crisp and brown.

Vegetables can be cooked in foil parcels as well as on kebab skewers. Slice them roughly, sprinkle with olive oil, herbs and seasonings and wrap tightly. Cook until tender.

STARTERS & SALADS

With so many fresh ingredients readily available,
it is very easy to create some deliciously different
starters and salads to make the perfect introduction
to a vegetarian meal. The ideas in this chapter are an
inspiration to cook and a treat to eat, and they give
an edge to the appetite that makes the main course
even more enjoyable.

When choosing a starter, make sure that you provide a
good balance of flavours, colours and textures that offer
variety and contrast. Balance the nature of the recipes
too - a rich main course is best preceded by a light
starter such as a salad, which is just enough to interest
the palate and stimulate the taste buds.

A salad also makes a refreshing accompaniment to the
main course. Or you could serve two or three together
as a complete meal - they are a good source of vitamins
and minerals. Always use the freshest possible
ingredients for maximum flavour and texture.

Cheese, Garlic & Herb Pâté

This wonderful soft cheese pâté is fragrant with the aroma of fresh herbs and garlic. Serve with triangles of Melba toast to make the perfect starter.

SERVES 4

INGREDIENTS

15 g/½ oz/1 tbsp butter
1 garlic clove, crushed
3 spring onions (scallions), chopped finely
125 g/4 oz/½ cup full-fat soft cheese
2 tbsp chopped mixed fresh herbs,
such as parsley, chives, marjoram,
oregano and basil
175 g/6 oz/1½ cups mature (sharp)
Cheddar, grated finely
pepper
4–6 slices of white bread
from a medium-cut sliced loaf
mixed salad leaves (greens) and cherry tomatoes,
to serve

TO GARNISH

ground paprika
sprigs of fresh herbs

1 Melt the butter in a small frying pan (skillet) and gently fry the garlic and spring onions (scallions) together for 3–4 minutes, until softened. Allow to cool.

2 Beat the soft cheese in a large mixing bowl, then add the garlic and spring onions (scallions). Stir in the herbs, mixing well.

3 Add the Cheddar and work the mixture together to form a stiff paste. Cover and chill until ready to serve.

4 To make the Melba toast, toast the slices of bread on both sides, and then cut off the crusts. Using a sharp bread knife, cut through the slices horizontally to make very thin slices. Cut into triangles and then lightly grill (broil) the untoasted sides.

5 Arrange the mixed salad leaves on 4 serving plates with the cherry tomatoes. Pile the cheese pâté on top and sprinkle with a little paprika. Garnish with sprigs of fresh herbs and serve with the Melba toast.

Step *2*

Step *3*

Step *4*

Herb, Toasted Nut & Paprika Cheese Nibbles

These tiny cheese balls are rolled in fresh herbs, toasted nuts or paprika to make tasty nibbles for parties, buffets, or pre-dinner drinks.

SERVES 4

INGREDIENTS

125 g/4 oz Ricotta
125 g/4 oz Double Gloucester (brick) cheese, grated finely
2 tsp chopped parsley
60 g/2 oz/½ cup chopped mixed nuts
3 tbsp chopped fresh herbs, such as parsley, chives, marjoram, lovage and chervil
2 tbsp mild paprika
pepper
sprigs of fresh herbs, to garnish

1 Mix together the Ricotta and Double Gloucester (brick) cheeses. Add the parsley and pepper, and work together until combined.

2 Form the mixture into small balls. Cover and chill for about 20 minutes to firm.

3 Scatter the chopped nuts on to a baking sheet and place them under a preheated grill (broiler) until lightly browned. Take care as they can easily burn. Leave them to cool.

4 Sprinkle the nuts, herbs and paprika into 3 separate small bowls. Divide the cheese balls into 3 equal piles and then roll 1 quantity in the nuts, 1 quantity in the herbs and 1 quantity in the paprika.

5 Arrange on a serving platter. Chill until ready to serve, and then garnish with sprigs of fresh herbs.

Step *1*

Step *2*

Step *3*

Avocado Cream Terrine

The smooth, rich taste of ripe avocados combines well with thick, creamy yogurt and single (light) cream to make this impressive terrine.

SERVES 6

INGREDIENTS

2 ripe avocados
4 tbsp cold water
2 tsp gelozone (vegetarian gelatine)
1 tbsp lemon juice
4 tbsp mayonnaise
150 ml /¼ pint/⅔ cup thick yogurt
150 ml /¼ pint/⅔ cup single (light) cream
salt and pepper
mixed salad leaves (greens), to serve

TO GARNISH

cucumber slices
nasturtium flowers

1 Peel the avocados and remove the stones (pits). Put in a blender or food processor, or a large bowl, with the water, gelozone (vegetarian gelatine), lemon juice, mayonnaise, yogurt, cream and seasoning.

2 Process for about 10–15 seconds, or beat by hand, until smooth.

3 Transfer the mixture to a small saucepan and heat gently, stirring constantly, until just boiling.

4 Pour the mixture into a 900 ml/1½ pint/3½ cup plastic food storage box or terrine. Allow to cool and set, and then refrigerate until chilled – about 1½ –2 hours.

5 Turn the mixture out of its container and cut into neat slices. Arrange a bed of salad leaves (greens) on 6 serving plates. Place a slice of avocado terrine on top and garnish with cucumber slices and nasturtium flowers.

Step *2*

Step *3*

Step *4*

Fiery Salsa with Tortilla Chips

Make this Mexican-style salsa to perk up jaded palates.
Its lively flavours really get the tastebuds going.

SERVES 6

INGREDIENTS

2 small red chillies
1 tbsp lime or lemon juice
2 large ripe avocados
5 cm/2 inch piece cucumber
2 tomatoes, peeled
1 small garlic clove, crushed
few drops of Tabasco sauce
salt and pepper
lime or lemon slices, to garnish
tortilla chips, to serve

1 Remove and discard the stem and seeds from 1 chilli. Chop very finely and place in a mixing bowl. To make a chilli 'flower' for garnish, slice the remaining chilli from the stem to the tip several times without removing the stem. Place in a bowl of cold water, so that the 'petals' open out.

2 Add the lime or lemon juice to the mixing bowl. Halve, stone (pit) and peel the avocados. Add to the mixing bowl and mash with a fork. (The lime or lemon juice prevents the avocado from turning brown.)

3 Chop the cucumber and tomatoes finely and add to the avocado mixture with the crushed garlic.

4 Season the dip to taste with Tabasco sauce, salt and pepper.

5 Transfer the dip to a serving bowl. Garnish with slices of lime or lemon and the chilli flower. Put the bowl on a large plate, surround with tortilla chips and serve.

Step *1*

Step *2*

Step *4*

Aubergine (Eggplant) Dipping Platter

Dipping platters are a very sociable dish, bringing together all the diners at the table. This substantial dip is served with vegetables as an appetizer.

SERVES 4

INGREDIENTS

1 aubergine (eggplant),
peeled and cut into 2.5 cm/1 inch cubes
3 tbsp sesame seeds,
roasted in a dry pan over a low heat
1 tsp sesame oil
grated rind and juice of ½ lime
1 small shallot, diced
½ tsp salt
1 tsp sugar
1 red chilli, deseeded and sliced
125 g/4 oz/1¼ cups broccoli florets
2 carrots, cut into matchsticks
125 g/4 oz/8 baby corn, cut in half lengthways
2 celery stalks, cut into matchsticks
1 baby red cabbage,
cut into 8 wedges, the leaves of each wedge
held together by the core

1 Cook the diced aubergine (eggplant) in boiling water for 7–8 minutes.

2 Meanwhile, grind the sesame seeds with the oil in a food processor or pestle and mortar.

3 Add the aubergine (eggplant), lime rind and juice, shallot, salt, sugar and chilli in that order to the sesame seeds. Process, or chop and mash by hand, until smooth.

4 Check the seasoning then spoon into a bowl. Serve surrounded by the broccoli, carrots, baby corn, celery and red cabbage.

Step *1*

Step *3*

Step *4*

Mint & Cannellini Bean Dip

*This dip is ideal for pre-dinner drinks or for handing around at a party,
accompanied by crisps and colourful vegetable crudités.*

SERVES 6

INGREDIENTS

175 g/6 oz/1 cup dried cannellini beans
1 small garlic clove, crushed
1 bunch spring onions (scallions),
chopped roughly
handful of fresh mint leaves
2 tbsp tahini (sesame seed paste)
2 tbsp olive oil
1 tsp ground cumin
1 tsp ground coriander
lemon juice
salt and pepper
sprigs of fresh mint, to garnish

TO SERVE

fresh vegetable crudités,
such as cauliflower florets, carrots,
cucumber, radishes and (bell) peppers

1 Soak the cannellini beans overnight in plenty of cold water.

2 Rinse and drain the beans, put them into a large saucepan and cover them with cold water. Bring to the boil and boil rapidly for 10 minutes. Reduce the heat, cover and simmer until tender.

3 Drain the beans and transfer them to a bowl or food processor. Add the garlic, spring onions (scallions), mint, tahini and olive oil.

4 Blend the mixture for about 15 seconds, or mash well by hand, until smooth.

5 Transfer the mixture to a bowl and season with cumin, coriander, lemon juice, salt and pepper, according to taste. Mix well, cover and leave in a cool place for 30 minutes to allow the flavours to develop.

6 Spoon the dip into serving bowls, garnish with sprigs of fresh mint and surround with vegetable crudités.

Step 3

Step 4

Step 5

(Bell) Peppers with Rosemary Baste

*The flavour of grilled (broiled) or roasted (bell) peppers is very different
from when they are eaten raw, so do try them cooked in this way.*

SERVES 4

INGREDIENTS

4 tbsp olive oil
finely grated rind of 1 lemon
4 tbsp lemon juice
1 tbsp balsamic vinegar
1 tbsp crushed fresh rosemary,
or 1 tsp dried rosemary
2 red (bell) peppers, halved,
cored and deseeded
2 yellow (bell) peppers, halved,
cored and deseeded
2 tbsp pine kernels (nuts)
salt and pepper
sprigs of fresh rosemary, to garnish

1 Mix together the olive oil, lemon rind, lemon juice, vinegar and rosemary. Season with salt and pepper.

2 Place the (bell) peppers, skin-side uppermost, on the rack of a grill (broiler) pan, lined with foil. Brush the olive oil mixture over them.

3 Cook the (bell) peppers until the skin begins to char, basting frequently with the lemon juice mixture. Remove from the heat, cover with foil to trap the steam and leave for 5 minutes.

4 Meanwhile, scatter the pine kernels (nuts) on to the grill (broiler) rack and toast them lightly.

5 Peel the (bell) peppers, slice them into strips and place them in a warmed serving dish. Sprinkle with the pine kernels and drizzle any remaining lemon juice mixture over them. Garnish with sprigs of fresh rosemary and serve at once.

Step *1*

Step *3*

Step *5*

Marinated Vegetable Salad

*Lightly steamed vegetables taste superb served slightly warm in a
marinade of olive oil, white wine, vinegar and fresh herbs.*

SERVES 4-6

INGREDIENTS

175 g/6 oz baby carrots, trimmed
2 celery hearts, cut into 4 pieces
125g/4 oz sugar snap peas
or mangetout (snow peas)
1 bulb fennel, sliced
175 g/6 oz small asparagus spears
15 g/½ oz/1½ tbsp sunflower seeds
sprigs of fresh dill, to garnish

DRESSING

4 tbsp olive oil
4 tbsp dry white wine
2 tbsp white wine vinegar
1 tbsp chopped fresh dill
1 tbsp chopped fresh parsley
salt and pepper

1 Steam the carrots, celery, sugar snap peas or mangetout (snow peas), fennel and asparagus over gently boiling water until just tender. It is important that they retain a little 'bite'.

2 Meanwhile, make the dressing. Mix together the olive oil, wine, vinegar and chopped herbs. Season well with salt and pepper.

3 When the vegetables are cooked, transfer them to a serving dish and pour over the dressing at once. The hot vegetables will absorb the flavour of the dressing as they cool.

4 Scatter the sunflower seeds on a baking sheet and toast them under a preheated grill (broiler) until lightly browned. Sprinkle them over the vegetables.

5 Serve the salad while the vegetables are still slightly warm, garnished with sprigs of fresh dill.

Step 1

Step 3

Step 4

Carrot & Cashew Nut Coleslaw

*This simple salad has a dressing made from poppy seeds
pan-fried in sesame oil to bring out their flavour.*

SERVES 4

INGREDIENTS

1 large carrot, grated
1 small onion, chopped finely
2 celery stalks, chopped
¼ small, hard white cabbage, shredded
1 tbsp chopped fresh parsley
4 tbsp sesame oil
½ tsp poppy seeds
60 g/2 oz/½ cup cashew nuts
2 tbsp white wine or cider vinegar
salt and pepper
sprigs of fresh parsley, to garnish

1 In a large salad bowl, mix together the carrot, onion, celery and cabbage. Stir in the chopped parsley and season with salt and pepper.

2 Heat the sesame oil in a saucepan with a lid. Add the poppy seeds and cover the pan. Cook over a medium-high heat until the seeds start to make a popping sound. Remove from the heat and leave to cool.

3 Scatter the cashew nuts on to a baking sheet. Place them under a medium-hot grill (broiler) and toast until lightly browned, being careful not to burn them. Leave to cool.

4 Add the vinegar to the oil and poppy seeds, then pour over the carrot mixture. Add the cooled cashew nuts. Toss together to coat with the dressing.

5 Garnish the salad with sprigs of parsley and serve.

Step *2*

Step *3*

Step *4*

Three-Way Potato Salad

*There's nothing to beat the flavour of new potatoes,
served just warm in a delicious dressing.*

SERVES 4

INGREDIENTS

500 g/1lb new potatoes for each dressing
fresh herbs, to garnish

LIGHT CURRY DRESSING

1 tbsp vegetable oil
1 tbsp medium curry paste
1 small onion, chopped
1 tbsp mango chutney, chopped
6 tbsp natural yogurt
3 tbsp single (light) cream
2 tbsp mayonnaise
salt and pepper
1 tbsp single (light) cream, to garnish

VINAIGRETTE DRESSING

6 tbsp hazelnut oil
3 tbsp cider vinegar
1 tsp wholegrain mustard
1 tsp caster (superfine) sugar
few basil leaves, torn into shreds
salt and pepper

PARSLEY, SPRING ONION (SCALLION) AND SOURED CREAM DRESSING

150 ml/¼ pint/⅔ cup soured cream
3 tbsp light mayonnaise
4 spring onions (scallions),
trimmed and chopped finely
1 tbsp chopped fresh parsley

1 To make the Light Curry Dressing, heat the vegetable oil in a saucepan and add the curry paste and onion. Fry together, stirring frequently, until the onion is soft. Remove from the heat and leave to cool slightly.

2 Mix together the mango chutney, yogurt, cream and mayonnaise. Add the curry mixture and blend together. Season with salt and pepper.

3 To make the Vinaigrette Dressing, whisk the hazelnut oil, cider vinegar, mustard, sugar and basil together in a small jug or bowl. Season with salt and pepper.

4 To make the Parsley, Spring Onion (Scallion) and Soured Cream Dressing, combine all the ingredients, mixing well. Season with salt and pepper.

5 Cook the potatoes in lightly salted boiling water until just tender. Drain well and leave to cool for 5 minutes, then add the chosen dressing, tossing to coat. Serve, garnished with fresh herbs, spooning a little single (light) cream on to the potatoes if you have used the curry dressing.

Step *1*

Step *2*

Step *4*

Three-Bean Salad

Fresh dwarf (thin) green beans are combined with soya beans and red kidney beans in a chive and tomato dressing, to make a tasty salad.

SERVES 4–6

INGREDIENTS

3 tbsp olive oil
1 tbsp lemon juice
1 tbsp tomato purée (paste)
1 tbsp light malt vinegar
1 tbsp chopped fresh chives
175 g/6 oz dwarf (thin) green beans
425 g/14 oz can soya beans,
rinsed and drained
425 g/14 oz can red kidney beans,
rinsed and drained
2 tomatoes, chopped
4 spring onions (scallions),
trimmed and chopped
125 g/4 oz Feta cheese, cut into cubes
salt and pepper
mixed salad leaves (greens), to serve
chopped fresh chives, to garnish

1 Put the olive oil, lemon juice, tomato purée, vinegar and chives into a large bowl and whisk together until thoroughly combined.

2 Cook the dwarf (thin) green beans in a little boiling, lightly salted water until just cooked, about 4–5 minutes. Drain, refresh under cold running water and drain again. Pat dry with paper towels.

3 Add the green beans, soya beans and red kidney beans to the dressing, stirring to mix.

4 Add the tomatoes, spring onions (scallions) and Feta cheese to the bean mixture, tossing gently to coat in the dressing. Season well with salt and pepper.

5 Arrange the mixed salad leaves on 4 serving plates. Pile the bean salad on to the plates and garnish with chopped chives.

 Step *1*

Step *3*

Step *4*

Red Onion, Cherry Tomato & Pasta Salad

Pasta tastes perfect in this lively salad, dressed with red wine vinegar, lemon juice, basil and olive oil.

SERVES 4

INGREDIENTS

175 g/6 oz/1½ cups pasta shapes
1 yellow (bell) pepper, halved,
cored and deseeded
2 small courgettes (zucchini), sliced
1 red onion, sliced thinly
125 g/4 oz cherry tomatoes, halved
handful of fresh basil leaves,
torn into small pieces
salt
sprigs of fresh basil, to garnish

DRESSING

4 tbsp olive oil
2 tbsp red wine vinegar
2 tsp lemon juice
1 tsp Dijon mustard
½ tsp caster (superfine) sugar
salt and pepper

1 Cook the pasta in plenty of boiling, lightly salted water for about 8 minutes, or until just tender.

2 Meanwhile, place the (bell) pepper halves, skin-side uppermost, under a preheated grill (broiler) until they just begin to char. Leave them to cool, then peel and slice them into strips.

3 Cook the courgettes (zucchini) in a small amount of boiling, lightly salted water for 3–4 minutes, until cooked, yet still crunchy. Drain and refresh under cold running water to cool quickly.

4 To make the dressing, mix together the olive oil, red wine vinegar, lemon juice, mustard and sugar. Season well with salt and pepper. Add the basil leaves.

5 Drain the pasta well and tip it into a large serving bowl. Add the dressing and toss well. Add the pepper, courgettes (zucchini), onion and cherry tomatoes, stirring to combine. Cover and leave at room temperature for about 30 minutes to allow the flavours to develop.

6 Serve, garnished with sprigs of fresh basil.

Step *1*

Step *2*

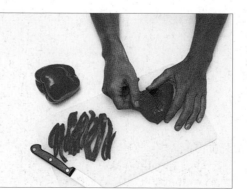

Step *4*

Moroccan Orange & Couscous Salad

*Couscous is a type of semolina made from durum wheat. It is wonderful
in salads as it readily takes up the flavour of the dressing.*

SERVES 4–6

INGREDIENTS

175 g/6 oz/2 cups couscous
1 bunch spring onions (scallions),
trimmed and chopped finely
1 small green (bell) pepper, cored,
deseeded and chopped
10 cm/4 inch piece cucumber, chopped
175 g/6 oz can chick-peas (garbanzo beans),
rinsed and drained
60 g/2 oz/⅔ cup sultanas
(golden raisins) or raisins
2 oranges
salt and pepper
lettuce leaves, to serve
sprigs of fresh mint, to garnish

DRESSING

finely grated rind of 1 orange
1 tbsp chopped fresh mint
150 ml/¼ pint/⅔ cup natural yogurt

1 Put the couscous into a bowl and cover with boiling water. Leave it to soak for about 15 minutes to swell the grains, then stir with a fork to separate them.

2 Add the spring onions (scallions), green (bell) pepper, cucumber, chick-peas (garbanzo beans) and sultanas (golden raisins) or raisins to the couscous, stirring to combine. Season well with salt and pepper.

3 To make the dressing, mix the orange rind, mint and yogurt. Pour over the couscous mixture and stir well.

4 Using a sharp serrated knife, remove the peel and pith from the oranges. Cut the flesh into segments, removing all the membrane.

5 Arrange the lettuce leaves on 4 serving plates. Divide the couscous mixture between the plates and arrange the orange segments on top. Garnish with sprigs of fresh mint and serve.

Step *1*

Step *2*

Step *4*

Goat's Cheese Salad

A delicious hot salad of melting goat's cheese over sliced tomato and basil on a base of hot ciabatta bread.

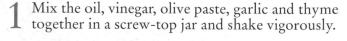

SERVES 4

INGREDIENTS

3 tbsp olive oil
1 tbsp white wine vinegar
1 tsp black olive paste
1 garlic clove, crushed
1 tsp chopped fresh thyme
1 ciabatta loaf
4 small tomatoes
12 fresh basil leaves
2 × 125 g/4 oz logs goat's cheese

TO SERVE

mixed salad leaves (greens) including rocket (arugula) and radicchio

1 Mix the oil, vinegar, olive paste, garlic and thyme together in a screw-top jar and shake vigorously.

2 Cut the ciabatta in half horizontally then in half vertically to make 4 pieces.

3 Drizzle some of the dressing over the bread then arrange the tomatoes and basil leaves over the top.

4 Cut each roll of goat's cheese into 6 slices and lay 3 slices on each piece of ciabatta.

5 Brush with some of the dressing and place in a preheated oven, 230°C/450°F/Gas Mark 8, for 5–6 minutes until turning brown at the edges.

6 Pour the remaining dressing over the mixed salad leaves (greens) and serve with the baked bread.

 Step *2*

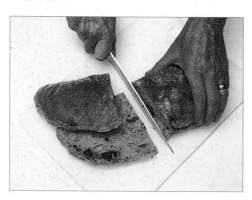

Step *3*

Step *4*

SOUPS

Soup must be one of the most satisfying foods
available. It produces a definite feeling of well-being
which can help lift fatigue, it is easy to digest but still
satisfying, and is ideal both for solitary meals or for
serving to crowds.

Soup is simple to make but always produces tasty results.
A wide range of ingredients can be used in addition to
vegetables - pulses (legumes), grains, noodles, cheese and
yogurt are all good candidates. It is easy to make
substitutions when you don't have certain
ingredients to hand.

There is an enormous variety of soups which you can
make with vegetables. They can be rich and creamy,
thick and chunky, light and delicate, and hot or chilled.
The vegetables are often puréed to give a smooth
consistency and thicken the soup, but you can also
purée just some of the mixture to give the soup
more texture and interest.

The secret of a good soup lies in using a well flavoured,
good quality stock as the base. Although there are some
excellent vegetable stock cubes available, it is a
homemade stock that gives the edge to any soup. You'll
find a recipe for Fresh Vegetable Stock on page 12.

Avocado & Mint Soup

A rich and creamy pale green soup made with avocados and enhanced by a touch of chopped mint. Serve chilled in summer or hot in winter.

SERVES 4-6

INGREDIENTS

45 g/1½ oz/3 tbsp butter or margarine
6 spring onions (scallions), sliced
1 garlic clove, crushed
30 g/1 oz/¼ cup plain (all-purpose) flour
600 ml/1 pint/2½ cups Fresh Vegetable
Stock (page 12)
2 ripe avocados
2–3 tsp lemon juice
good pinch of grated lemon rind
150 ml/¼ pint/⅔ cup milk
150 ml/¼ pint/⅔ cup single (light) cream
1–1½ tbsp chopped fresh mint
salt and pepper
sprigs of fresh mint, to garnish

MINTED GARLIC BREAD

125 g/4 oz/½ cup butter
1–2 tbsp chopped fresh mint
1–2 garlic cloves, crushed
1 wholemeal (whole wheat)
or white French bread stick

1 Melt the butter or margarine in a large saucepan, add the spring onions (scallions) and garlic and fry gently for about 3 minutes until soft but not coloured.

2 Stir in the flour and cook for a minute or so. Gradually stir in the stock then bring to the boil. Leave to simmer gently while preparing the avocados.

3 Peel the avocados, discard the stones (pits) and chop coarsely. Add to the soup with the lemon juice and rind and seasoning. Cover and simmer for about 10 minutes until tender.

4 Cool the soup slightly then press through a sieve (strainer) or blend in a food processor or blender until smooth. Pour into a bowl.

5 Stir in the milk and cream, adjust the seasoning, then stir in the mint. Cover and chill thoroughly.

6 To make the minted garlic bread, soften the butter and beat in the mint and garlic. Cut the loaf into slanting slices but leave a hinge on the bottom crust. Spread each slice with the butter and reassemble the loaf. Wrap in foil and place in a preheated oven, 180°C/ 350°F/Gas Mark 4, for about 15 minutes.

7 Serve the soup garnished with a sprig of mint and accompanied by the minted garlic bread.

Step *2*

Step *3*

Step *5*

Gazpacho

This Spanish soup is full of chopped and grated vegetables with a puréed tomato base. Serve with extra chopped vegetables and croûtons.

SERVES 4

INGREDIENTS

½ small cucumber
½ small green (bell) pepper, chopped very finely
500 g/1 lb ripe tomatoes, peeled or
425 g/14 oz can chopped tomatoes
½ onion, chopped coarsely
2–3 garlic cloves, crushed
3 tbsp olive oil
2 tbsp white wine vinegar
1–2 tbsp lemon or lime juice
2 tbsp tomato purée (paste)
450 ml/¾ pint/scant 2 cups tomato juice
salt and pepper

TO SERVE

chopped green (bell) pepper
thinly sliced onion rings
garlic croûtons

1 Coarsely grate the cucumber into a bowl and add the chopped green (bell) pepper.

2 Blend the tomatoes, onion and garlic in a food processor or blender, then add the oil, vinegar, lemon or lime juice and tomato purée (paste) and blend until smooth. Alternatively, finely chop the tomatoes and finely grate the onion, then mix both with the garlic, oil, vinegar, lemon or lime juice and tomato purée (paste).

3 Add the tomato mixture to the cucumber and green (bell) pepper and mix well, then add the tomato juice and mix again.

4 Season to taste, cover the bowl with clingfilm (plastic wrap) and chill thoroughly – for at least 6 hours and preferably longer for the flavours to meld together.

5 Prepare the side dishes of green (bell) pepper, onion rings and garlic croûtons, and arrange in individual serving bowls.

6 Ladle the soup into bowls, preferably from a soup tureen set on the table with the side dishes around it. Hand the dishes around to allow the guests to help themselves.

Step *2*

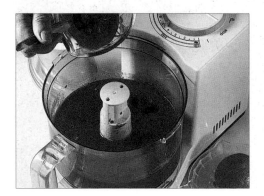

Step *3*

Step *5*

Vichyssoise

This is a classic creamy soup made from potatoes and leeks. To achieve the delicate pale colour, be sure to use only the white parts of the leeks.

SERVES 4–6

INGREDIENTS

3 large leeks
45 g/1½ oz/3 tbsp butter or margarine
1 onion, sliced thinly
500 g/1 lb potatoes, chopped
900 ml/1½ pints/3½ cups Fresh Vegetable
Stock (page 12)
2 tsp lemon juice
pinch of ground nutmeg
¼ tsp ground coriander
1 bay leaf
1 egg yolk
150 ml/¼ pint/⅔ cup single (light) cream
salt and white pepper

TO GARNISH

snipped chives or crisply fried
and crumbled bacon

1 Trim the leeks and remove most of the green part (it can be served as a vegetable). Slice the white part of the leeks very finely.

2 Melt the butter or margarine in a saucepan and gently fry the leeks and onion for about 5 minutes without browning, stirring from time to time.

3 Add the potatoes, stock, lemon juice, seasoning, nutmeg, coriander and bay leaf to the pan and bring to the boil. Cover and simmer for about 30 minutes until all the vegetables are very soft.

4 Cool the soup a little, discard the bay leaf and then press through a sieve (strainer) or blend in a food processor or blender until smooth. Pour into a clean pan.

5 Blend the egg yolk into the cream, add a little of the soup to the mixture and then whisk it all back into the soup and reheat gently without boiling. Adjust seasoning to taste. Cool and chill thoroughly.

6 Serve the soup sprinkled with snipped chives or crisply fried and crumbled bacon.

Step *1*

Step *2*

Step *5*

Noodle, Mushroom & Ginger Soup

*Thai soups are very quickly and easily put together, and are cooked so
that each ingredient can still be tasted in the finished dish.*

SERVES 4

INGREDIENTS

15 g/½ oz/¼ cup dried Chinese mushrooms
or 125 g/4 oz/1⅓ cups field
or chestnut (crimini) mushrooms
1 litre/1¾ pints/4 cups hot Fresh Vegetable
Stock (page 12)
125 g/4 oz thread egg noodles
2 tsp sunflower oil
3 garlic cloves, crushed
2.5 cm/1 inch piece ginger, shredded finely
½ tsp mushroom ketchup
1 tsp light soy sauce
125 g/4 oz/2 cups bean-sprouts
coriander (cilantro) leaves, to garnish

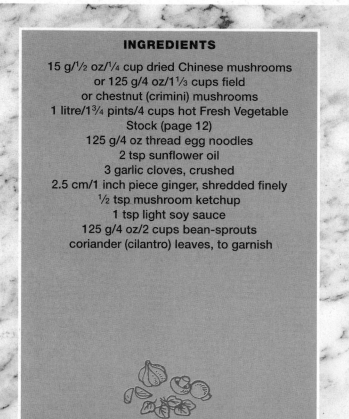

1 Soak the dried Chinese mushrooms, if using, for at
least 30 minutes in 300 ml/½ pint/1¼ cups of the hot
vegetable stock. Remove the stalks and discard, then slice
the mushrooms. Reserve the stock.

2 Cook the noodles for 2–3 minutes in boiling water.
Drain and rinse. Set them aside.

3 Heat the oil over a high heat in a wok or large, heavy
frying pan (skillet). Add the garlic and ginger, stir and
add the mushrooms. Stir over a high heat for 2 minutes.

4 Add the remaining vegetable stock with the reserved
stock and bring to the boil. Add the mushroom
ketchup and soy sauce.

5 Stir in the bean-sprouts. Cook until tender and serve
immediately over the noodles, garnished with
coriander (cilantro) leaves.

Step *2*

Step *4*

Step *5*

Beetroot Soup

*Here are two variations using the same vegetable: a creamy soup made
with puréed cooked beetroot; and a traditional clear soup, Bortsch.*

SERVES 4–6

INGREDIENTS

BORTSCH

500 g/1 lb raw beetroot, peeled and grated
2 carrots, chopped finely
1 large onion, chopped finely
1 garlic clove, crushed
1 bouquet garni
1 litre/2 pints/5 cups Fresh Vegetable
Stock (page 12)
2–3 tsp lemon juice
salt and pepper
150 ml/¼ pint/⅔ cup soured cream, to serve

CREAMED BEETROOT SOUP

60 g/2 oz/¼ cup butter or margarine
2 large onions, chopped finely
1–2 carrots, chopped
2 celery sticks, chopped
500 g/1 lb cooked beetroot, diced
1–2 tbsp lemon juice
900 ml/1½ pints/3½ cups Fresh Vegetable
Stock (page 12)
300 ml/½ pint/1¼ cups milk
salt and pepper

TO SERVE

grated cooked beetroot
or 6 tbsp soured or double (heavy) cream,
lightly whipped

1 To make bortsch, place the beetroot, carrots, onion, garlic, bouquet garni, stock, lemon juice and seasoning in a saucepan. Bring to the boil, cover and simmer for 45 minutes.

2 Press the soup through a fine sieve (strainer) or a sieve (strainer) lined with muslin (cheesecloth), then pour into a clean pan. Adjust the seasoning and add extra lemon juice if necessary.

3 Bring to the boil and simmer for 1–2 minutes. Serve with a spoonful of soured cream swirled through.

4 To make creamed beetroot soup, melt the butter or margarine in a saucepan and fry the onions, carrots and celery until just beginning to colour.

5 Add the beetroot, 1 tablespoon of the lemon juice, the stock and seasoning and bring to the boil. Cover and simmer for 30 minutes until tender.

6 Cool slightly, then press through a sieve (strainer) or blend in a food processor or blender. Pour into a clean pan. Add the milk and bring to the boil. Adjust the seasoning, add extra lemon juice if necessary. Top with grated beetroot or soured or double (heavy) cream.

 Step *1*

 Step *2*

Step *5*

Cream Cheese & Fresh Herb Soup

*Make the most of home-grown herbs to create this wonderfully creamy soup
with its marvellous garden-fresh fragrance.*

SERVES 4

INGREDIENTS

30 g/1 oz/2 tbsp butter or margarine
2 onions, chopped
900 ml/1½ pints/3½ cups Fresh Vegetable
Stock (page 12)
30 g/1 oz coarsely chopped mixed fresh herbs,
such as parsley, chives, thyme, basil and oregano
200 g/7 oz/1 cup full-fat soft cheese
1 tbsp cornflour (cornstarch)
1 tbsp milk
chopped fresh chives, to garnish

1 Melt the butter or margarine in a large saucepan and add the onions. Fry for 2 minutes, then cover and turn the heat to low. Allow the onions to cook gently for 5 minutes, then remove the lid.

2 Add the stock and herbs to the saucepan. Bring to the boil, then turn down the heat. Cover and simmer gently for 20 minutes.

3 Remove the saucepan from the heat. Blend the soup in a food processor or blender for about 15 seconds, until smooth. Alternatively, press it through a sieve (strainer). Return the soup to the saucepan.

4 Reserve a little of the cheese for garnish. Spoon the remaining cheese into the soup and whisk until the cheese is incorporated.

5 Mix the cornflour (cornstarch) with the milk, then stir into the soup and heat, stirring constantly, until thickened and smooth.

6 Pour the soup into 4 warmed bowls. Spoon some of the reserved cheese into each bowl and garnish with chives. Serve at once.

Step *1*

Step *2*

Step *4*

Gardener's Broth

This thick, hearty soup uses a variety of green vegetables with a flavouring of ground coriander. A finishing touch of thinly sliced leeks adds texture.

SERVES 4–6

INGREDIENTS

45 g/1½ oz/3 tbsp butter or margarine
1 onion, chopped
1–2 garlic cloves, crushed
1 large leek
250 g/8 oz Brussels sprouts
125 g/4 oz French (green) or runner beans
1.1 litres/2 pints/5 cups Fresh Vegetable Stock (page 12)
125 g/4 oz/¾ cup frozen peas
1 tbsp lemon juice
½ tsp ground coriander
4 tbsp double (heavy) cream
salt and pepper

MELBA TOAST

4–6 slices white bread

1 Melt the butter or margarine in a saucepan, add the onion and garlic and fry very gently, stirring occasionally, until they begin to soften but not colour.

2 Slice the white part of the leek very thinly and reserve; slice the remaining leeks. Slice the Brussels sprouts and thinly slice the beans.

3 Add the green part of the leeks, the Brussels sprouts and beans to the saucepan. Add the stock and bring to the boil. Simmer for 10 minutes.

4 Add the frozen peas, seasoning, lemon juice and coriander and continue to simmer for 10–15 minutes until the vegetables are tender.

5 Cool the soup a little, then press through a sieve (strainer) or blend in a food processor or blender until smooth. Pour into a clean pan.

6 Add the reserved slices of leek to the soup, bring back to the boil and simmer for about 5 minutes until the leeks are tender. Adjust the seasoning, stir in the cream and reheat gently.

7 Make the melba toast. Toast the bread on both sides under a preheated grill (broiler). Cut horizontally through the slices then toast the uncooked sides until they curl up. Serve immediately with the soup.

 Step 3

 Step 6

Step 7

Pumpkin Soup

This is an American classic that has now become popular worldwide.
When pumpkin is out of season use butternut squash in its place.

SERVES 4–6

INGREDIENTS

about 1 kg/2 lb pumpkin
45 g/1½ oz/3 tbsp butter or margarine
1 onion, sliced thinly
1 garlic clove, crushed
900 ml/1½ pints/3½ cups Fresh Vegetable
Stock (page 12)
½ tsp ground ginger
1 tbsp lemon juice
3–4 thinly pared strips of orange rind (optional)
1–2 bay leaves or 1 bouquet garni
300 ml/½ pint/1¼ cups milk
salt and pepper

TO GARNISH

4–6 tablespoons single (light)
or double (heavy) cream,
natural yogurt or fromage frais
snipped fresh chives

1 Peel the pumpkin, remove the seeds and then cut the flesh into 2.5 cm/1 inch cubes.

2 Melt the butter or margarine in a large saucepan, add the onion and garlic and fry gently until soft but not coloured.

3 Add the pumpkin and toss with the onion for a few minutes.

4 Add the stock and bring to the boil. Add the seasoning, ginger, lemon juice, strips of orange rind, if using, and bay leaves or bouquet garni. Cover and simmer gently for about 20 minutes until the pumpkin is very tender.

5 Discard the orange rind, if using, and the bay leaves or bouquet garni. Cool the soup a little and then press through a sieve (strainer) or blend in a food processor or blender until smooth. Pour into a clean saucepan.

6 Add the milk and reheat gently. Adjust the seasoning. Garnish with a swirl of cream, natural yogurt or fromage frais and snipped chives, and serve.

Step *1*

Step *5*

Step *6*

Chick-Pea (Garbanzo Bean) & Tomato Soup

*A thick vegetable soup which is a delicious meal in itself. Serve the soup
with thin shavings of Parmesan and warm ciabatta bread.*

SERVES 4

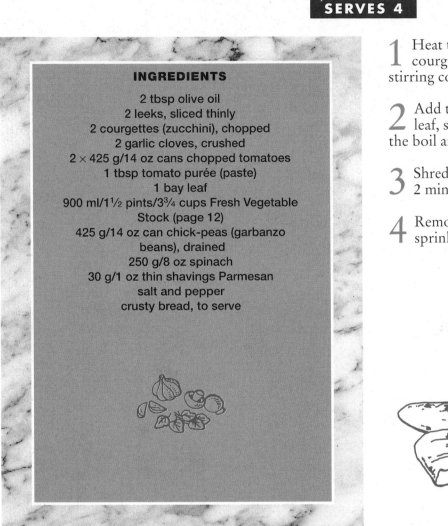

INGREDIENTS

2 tbsp olive oil
2 leeks, sliced thinly
2 courgettes (zucchini), chopped
2 garlic cloves, crushed
2 × 425 g/14 oz cans chopped tomatoes
1 tbsp tomato purée (paste)
1 bay leaf
900 ml/1½ pints/3¾ cups Fresh Vegetable
Stock (page 12)
425 g/14 oz can chick-peas (garbanzo
beans), drained
250 g/8 oz spinach
30 g/1 oz thin shavings Parmesan
salt and pepper
crusty bread, to serve

1 Heat the oil in a saucepan, add the leeks and
courgettes (zucchini) and cook briskly for 5 minutes,
stirring constantly.

2 Add the garlic, tomatoes, tomato purée (paste), bay
leaf, stock and chick-peas (garbanzo beans). Bring to
the boil and simmer for 5 minutes.

3 Shred the spinach finely, add to the soup and boil for
2 minutes. Season to taste.

4 Remove the bay leaf. Pour into a soup tureen and
sprinkle over the Parmesan. Serve with crusty bread.

Step *1*

Step *2*

Step *4*

Hot & Sour Soup

A very traditional staple of the Thai national diet, this soup is sold on street corners, at food bars and by mobile vendors all over the country.

SERVES 4

INGREDIENTS

1 tbsp sunflower oil
250 g/8 oz smoked tofu
(bean curd), sliced
90 g/3 oz/1 cup shiitake
mushrooms, sliced
2 tbsp chopped fresh coriander (cilantro)
125 g/4 oz/2 cups watercress
1 red chilli, sliced finely, to garnish

STOCK

1 tbsp tamarind pulp
2 dried red chillies, chopped
2 kaffir lime leaves, torn in half
2.5 cm/1 inch piece ginger root, chopped
5 cm/2 inch piece galangal, chopped
1 stalk lemon grass, chopped
1 onion, quartered
1 litre/1¾ pints/4 cups cold water

1 Put all the ingredients for the stock into a saucepan and bring to the boil. Simmer for 5 minutes. Remove from the heat and strain, reserving the stock.

2 Heat the oil in a wok or large, heavy frying pan (skillet) and cook the tofu (bean curd) over a high heat for about 2 minutes, stirring constantly. Pour in the strained stock.

3 Add the mushrooms and coriander (cilantro), and boil for 3 minutes. Add the watercress and boil for 1 minute more. Serve at once, garnished with chilli slices.

Step *1*

Step *2*

Step *3*

SNACKS & LIGHT MEALS

The ability to rustle up a simple snack or a quickly-prepared light meal can be very important in our busy lives. Sometimes we may not feel like eating a full-scale meal but nevertheless want something appetizing and satisfying. Or if lunch or dinner is going to be served very late, then we may want something to tide us over. Whether it is for a sustaining snack to break the day, or hearty nibbles to serve with pre-dinner drinks or as a starter, or an informal lunch or supper party, you'll find a mouthwatering collection of recipes in this chapter. They cater for all tastes and times of day, many can be prepared ahead of time and will not detain you in the kitchen for too long.

Try Greek Feta Croûtes (page 72) - a colourful and aromatic hot sandwich ideal for a speedy lunch, or serve mouthwatering Mediterranean Vegetable Tart (page 96) as a late night supper. With such a versatile selection to choose from, with a wide range of exciting flavours and ingredients, even the hungriest meat-eater will be satisfied.

Greek Feta Croûtes

*This is a wonderfully colourful and aromatic hot sandwich idea that
makes a good first course or light lunch dish.*

SERVES 6

INGREDIENTS

150 ml/¼ pint/⅔ cup olive oil
1 large clove garlic, crushed
1 tsp chopped fresh thyme
1 tbsp lemon juice
1 small aubergine (eggplant),
sliced, then cut into bite-sized pieces
1 large courgette (zucchini), thickly sliced
1 small bulb fennel,
sliced and cut into bite-sized chunks
1 small red pepper, cored,
deseeded and cut into pieces
1 small yellow pepper, cored,
deseeded and cut into pieces
1 onion, cut into thin wedges
4 large thick slices
country-style white crusty bread
125 g/4 oz Greek cheese (Halloumi or Feta,
for example), sliced or broken into pieces
salt and pepper
8 pitted black olives, cut into strips, to garnish

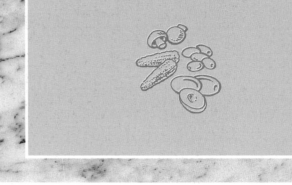

1 In a large bowl, beat the oil with the garlic, thyme, lemon juice, and salt and pepper to taste.

2 Add the prepared aubergine (eggplant), courgette (zucchini), fennel, peppers and onion, mixing well. Cover and leave to stand for about 1 hour, stirring occasionally.

3 Spread the vegetable mixture on a grill pan or baking sheet (cookie sheet) with upturned edges. Cook under a preheated moderate grill (broiler) for about 15 minutes, turning over frequently, until the vegetables are tender and lightly charred around the edges. Keep warm.

4 Meanwhile, brush the bread with a little of the cooking juices from the vegetables and toast lightly on both sides until just crisp and golden.

5 Top each slice of bread with the cheese, then cover with the cooked vegetable mixture.

6 Return to the grill (broiler) and cook for a further 3–5 minutes or until the cheese is bubbly. Serve at once, garnished with the black olive strips.

Step *3*

Step *4*

Step *5*

Walnut Finger Sandwich

Even the simplest sandwiches can be given a new twist if you make them with an unusual bread, such as the nut bread used here.

SERVES 1

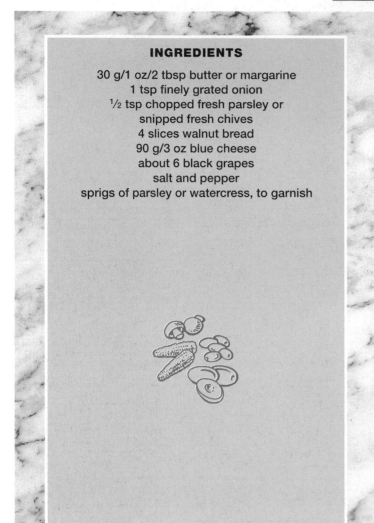

INGREDIENTS

30 g/1 oz/2 tbsp butter or margarine
1 tsp finely grated onion
½ tsp chopped fresh parsley or
snipped fresh chives
4 slices walnut bread
90 g/3 oz blue cheese
about 6 black grapes
salt and pepper
sprigs of parsley or watercress, to garnish

1 Beat the butter with the grated onion and parsley or chives to make a smooth spread. Season to taste with salt and pepper.

2 Spread the slices of bread with the prepared butter.

3 Slice the blue cheese thinly and layer the cheese on to two of the slices of bread so that the pieces of cheese overlap slightly.

4 Halve the grapes and remove any seeds. Place on top of the cheese slices, cut sides down.

5 Cover with the remaining slices of bread and press gently to seal.

6 Cut into thick finger sandwiches to serve. Garnish with parsley or watercress.

7 A blue cheese is the best companion for the nutty bread and grapes in this recipe. If you do not like blue cheese, replace it with a hard cheese with a sharp flavour, such as Cheddar.

Step *1*

Step *3*

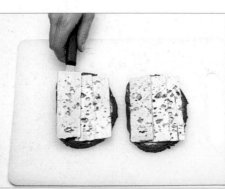

Step *4*

Vegetarian Munch & Crunch

Vegetarian lunch-boxes needn't resemble rabbit-food boxes if a selection of fruit, vegetables and dairy products is mixed imaginatively.

MAKES 2

INGREDIENTS

60 g/2 oz smooth peanut butter
60 g/2 oz/¼ cup full-fat soft cheese
1 small carrot
1 celery stick
4 green olives
small handful of alfalfa sprouts or bean-sprouts
½ small red apple
2 tsp lemon juice
2 large wholemeal (whole wheat)
rolls or baps (buns)

1 In a small bowl mix the peanut butter with the soft cheese to make a smooth spread.

2 Grate the carrot, finely chop the celery and dice the olives. Add to the spread and, using a wooden spoon, mix gently but thoroughly to combine.

3 Place the alfalfa sprouts or bean-sprouts in another bowl. Core but do not peel the apple, then dice. Add to the sprouts with the lemon juice and toss well to mix.

4 Cut the rolls or baps (buns) in half and spread each half generously with the vegetable, peanut butter and soft cheese mixture.

5 Top each roll with half of the sprout-and-apple mixture, replace the lids and press gently to seal.

Step *1*

Step *3*

Step *5*

Ricotta & Spinach Parcels

Ricotta and spinach make a great flavour combination, especially when encased in light puff-pastry parcels.

SERVES 4

INGREDIENTS

350 g/12 oz/3 cups spinach,
trimmed and washed thoroughly
30 g/1 oz/2 tbsp butter
1 small onion, chopped finely
1 tsp green peppercorns
500 g/1 lb puff pastry
250 g/8 oz/1 cup Ricotta
1 egg, beaten
salt
sprigs of fresh herbs, to garnish
fresh vegetables, to serve

1 Pack the spinach into a large saucepan. Add a little salt and a very small amount of water and cook until wilted. Drain well, cool and then squeeze out any excess moisture with the back of a spoon. Chop roughly.

2 Melt the butter in a small saucepan and fry the onion gently until softened, but not browned. Add the green peppercorns and cook for 2 more minutes. Remove from the heat, add the spinach and mix together.

3 Roll out the puff pastry thinly on a lightly floured work surface and cut into 4 squares, each 18 cm/7 inches across. Place a quarter of the spinach mixture in the centre of each square and top with a quarter of the cheese.

4 Brush a little beaten egg around the edges of the pastry squares and bring the corners together to form parcels. Press the edges together firmly to seal. Lift the parcels on to a greased baking sheet, brush with beaten egg and bake in a preheated oven, 200°C/ 400°F/Gas Mark 6, for 20–25 minutes, until risen and golden brown.

5 Serve hot, garnished with sprigs of fresh herbs and accompanied by fresh vegetables.

 1

 3

 4

Cauliflower Roulade

*A light-as-air mixture of eggs and vegetables produces a stylish
vegetarian dish that can be enjoyed hot or cold.*

SERVES 6

INGREDIENTS

1 small cauliflower, divided into florets
4 eggs, separated
90 g/3 oz/³⁄₄ cup mature (sharp) Cheddar, grated
60 g/2 oz/¹⁄₄ cup cottage cheese
large pinch of grated nutmeg
¹⁄₂ tsp mustard powder
salt and pepper

FILLING

1 bunch watercress, trimmed
60 g/2 oz/¹⁄₄ cup butter
30 g/1 oz/¹⁄₄ cup flour
175 ml/6 fl oz/³⁄₄ cup natural yogurt
30 g/1 oz/¹⁄₄ cup Cheddar, grated
60 g/2 oz/¹⁄₄ cup cottage cheese

1 Line a Swiss roll tin (pan) with baking parchment.

2 Steam the cauliflower until just tender. Drain under cold water to prevent further cooking. Put the cauliflower in a food processor and finely process, or chop and push through a sieve (strainer).

3 Beat the egg yolks, then stir in the cauliflower, 60 g/2 oz/¹⁄₂ cup of the Cheddar and the cottage cheese. Season with nutmeg, mustard, and salt and pepper. Whisk the egg whites until stiff but not dry, then fold into the cauliflower mixture, using a metal spoon.

4 Spread the mixture evenly in the prepared tin (pan) and bake in the preheated oven, 200°C/400°F/Gas6, for 20–25 minutes, until well risen and golden brown.

5 Finely chop the watercress, reserving a few sprigs for garnish. Melt the butter in a small pan and add the watercress. Cook for 3 minutes, stirring, until it has wilted. Blend in the flour, then stir in the yogurt and simmer for 2 minutes. Stir in the cheeses.

6 Turn out the roulade on to a damp tea towel (dish cloth) covered with baking parchment. Peel off the paper and leave for a minute to allow the steam to escape. Roll up the roulade, including a new sheet of paper, starting from one narrow end.

7 Unroll the roulade, spread the filling to within 2.5 cm/ 1 inch of the edges, and roll up. Transfer to a baking sheet (cookie sheet), sprinkle on the remaining Cheddar and return to the oven for 5 minutes. Serve hot or cold.

Step *4*

Step *6*

Step *7*

Creamy Mushroom Vol-au-Vent

A simple mixture of creamy, tender mushrooms filling a crisp, rich pastry case, this dish will make an impression at any dinner party.

SERVES 4

INGREDIENTS

500 g/1 lb puff pastry, thawed if frozen
1 egg, beaten, for glazing

FILLING

30 g/1 oz/2 tbsp butter or margarine
750 g/1½ lb mixed mushrooms such as open cup,
field, button, chestnut, shiitake,
pied de mouton, sliced
6 tbsp dry white wine
4 tbsp double (heavy) cream
2 tbsp chopped fresh chervil
salt and pepper
sprigs of fresh chervil, to garnish

1 Roll out the pastry on a lightly floured surface to a 20 cm/8 inch square.

2 Using a sharp knife, mark a square 2.5 cm/1 inch from the pastry edge, cutting halfway through the pastry.

3 Score the top in a diagonal pattern. Knock up the edges with a kitchen knife and put on a baking sheet (cookie sheet). Brush the top with beaten egg, taking care not to let the egg run into the cut. Bake in a preheated oven, 220°C/ 425°F/Gas Mark 7, for 35 minutes.

4 Cut out the central square. Discard the soft pastry inside the case, leaving the base intact. Return to the oven, with the square, for 10 minutes.

5 Meanwhile, make the filling. Melt the butter or margarine in a frying pan (skillet) and stir-fry the mushrooms over a high heat for 3 minutes.

6 Add the wine and cook for 10 minutes, stirring occasionally, until the mushrooms have softened. Stir in the cream, chervil and seasoning. Pile into the pastry case. Top with the pastry square, garnish and serve.

Step *3*

Step *4*

Step *6*

Goat's Cheese with Walnuts in Warm Oil & Vinegar Dressing

This delicious salad combines soft goat's cheese with walnut halves, served on a bed of mixed salad leaves (greens).

SERVES 4

INGREDIENTS

90 g/3 oz/1 cup walnut halves
mixed salad leaves (greens)
125 g/4 oz soft goat's cheese
snipped fresh chives, to garnish

DRESSING

6 tbsp walnut oil
3 tbsp white wine vinegar
1 tbsp clear honey
1 tsp Dijon mustard
pinch of ground ginger
salt and pepper

1 To make the dressing, whisk together the walnut oil, wine vinegar, honey, mustard and ginger in a small saucepan. Season to taste.

2 Heat the dressing gently, stirring occasionally, until warm. Add the walnut halves and continue to heat for 3–4 minutes.

3 Arrange the salad leaves on 4 serving plates and place spoonfuls of goat's cheese on top. Lift the walnut halves from the dressing with a perforated spoon, and scatter them over the salads.

4 Transfer the warm dressing to a small jug. Sprinkle chives over the salads and serve with the dressing.

Step *2*

Step *3*

Step *4*

Leek & Sun-Dried Tomato Timbales

Angel-hair pasta, known as cappellini, is mixed with fried leeks, sun-dried tomatoes, fresh oregano and beaten eggs, and baked in ramekins.

SERVES 4

INGREDIENTS

90 g/3 oz angel-hair pasta (cappellini)
30 g/1 oz/2 tbsp butter
1 tbsp olive oil
1 large leek, sliced finely
60 g/2 oz/½ cup sun-dried tomatoes in oil,
drained and chopped
1 tbsp chopped fresh oregano
or 1 tsp dried oregano
2 eggs, beaten
90 ml/3½ fl oz/generous ⅓ cup
single (light) cream
1 tbsp freshly grated Parmesan
salt and pepper
sprigs of oregano, to garnish
lettuce leaves, to serve

SAUCE

1 small onion, chopped finely
1 small garlic clove, crushed
350 g/12 oz tomatoes, peeled and chopped
1 tsp mixed dried Italian herbs
4 tbsp dry white wine

1 Cook the pasta in plenty of boiling salted water for about 3 minutes until al dente (just tender). Drain and rinse with cold water to cool quickly.

2 Meanwhile, heat the butter and oil in a frying pan (skillet). Gently fry the leek until softened, about 5–6 minutes. Add the sun-dried tomatoes and oregano, and cook for a further 2 minutes. Remove from the heat.

3 Add the leek mixture to the pasta. Stir in the beaten eggs, cream and Parmesan. Season with salt and pepper. Divide between 4 greased ramekin dishes or dariole moulds.

4 Place the dishes in a roasting tin with enough warm water to come halfway up their sides. Bake in a preheated oven, 180°C/350°F/Gas Mark 4, for about 30 minutes, until set.

5 To make the tomato sauce, fry the onion and garlic in the remaining butter and oil until softened. Add the tomatoes, herbs and wine. Cover and cook gently for about 20 minutes until pulpy. Blend in a food processor until smooth, or press through a sieve.

6 Run a knife or small spatula around the edge of the ramekin dishes, then turn out the timbales on to 4 warmed serving plates. Pour over a little sauce and garnish with sprigs of oregano. Serve with the lettuce leaves.

Step 2

Step 5

Step 6

Tofu (Bean Curd) & Vegetable Mini-Kebabs

Cubes of smoked tofu (bean curd) are speared on bamboo satay sticks with crisp vegetables, basted with lemon juice and olive oil, and then grilled.

SERVES 6

INGREDIENTS

300 g/10 oz smoked tofu (bean curd), cut into cubes
1 large red and 1 large yellow (bell) pepper, deseeded and cut into small squares
175 g/6 oz button mushrooms, wiped
1 small courgette (zucchini), sliced
finely grated rind and juice of 1 lemon
3 tbsp olive oil
1 tbsp chopped fresh parsley
1 tsp caster (superfine) sugar
salt and pepper
sprigs of parsley, to garnish

SAUCE

125 g/4 oz/1 cup cashew nuts
15 g/$^1/_3$ oz/1 tbsp butter
1 garlic clove, crushed
1 shallot, chopped finely
1 tsp ground coriander
1 tsp ground cumin
1 tbsp caster (superfine) sugar
1 tbsp desiccated (shredded) coconut
150 ml /$^1/_2$ pint/$^2/_3$ cup natural yogurt

1 Thread the tofu (bean curd) cubes, (bell) peppers, mushrooms and courgettes (zucchini) on to bamboo satay sticks. Arrange them in a shallow dish.

2 Mix together the lemon rind and juice, oil, parsley and sugar. Season well with salt and pepper. Pour over the kebabs, and brush them with the mixture. Leave for 10 minutes.

3 To make the sauce, scatter the cashew nuts on to a baking sheet and toast them until lightly browned.

4 Melt the butter in a saucepan and cook the garlic and shallot gently until softened. Transfer to a blender or food processor and add the nuts, coriander, cumin, sugar, coconut and yogurt. Blend until combined, about 15 seconds. Alternatively, chop the nuts very finely and mix with the remaining ingredients.

5 Place the kebabs under a preheated grill (broiler) and cook, turning and basting with the lemon juice mixture, until lightly browned. Garnish with sprigs of parsley, and serve with the cashew nut sauce.

 Step *1*

 Step *2*

Step *4*

Spinach Pancakes

*Serve these pancakes as a light lunch or supper dish, with a tomato
and basil salad for a dramatic colour contrast.*

SERVES 4

INGREDIENTS

90 g/3 oz/³⁄₄ cup wholemeal
(whole wheat) flour
1 egg
150 ml/¹⁄₄ pint/²⁄₃ cup natural yogurt
3 tbsp water
1 tbsp vegetable oil, plus extra for brushing
200 g/7 oz frozen leaf spinach,
defrosted and liquidized
pinch of grated nutmeg
salt and pepper

TO GARNISH

lemon wedges
fresh coriander (cilantro) sprigs

FILLING

1 tbsp vegetable oil
3 spring onions (scallions), thinly sliced
250 g/8 oz/1 cup Ricotta
4 tbsp natural yogurt
90 g/3 oz/³⁄₄ cup Gruyère, grated
1 egg, lightly beaten
125 g/4 oz/1 cup unsalted cashew nuts
2 tbsp chopped fresh parsley
pinch of cayenne pepper

1 Sift the flour and salt into a bowl and tip in any bran remaining in the sieve. Beat together the egg, yogurt, water and oil. Gradually pour it on to the flour, beating all the time. Stir in the spinach purée and season with pepper and nutmeg.

2 To make the filling, heat the oil in a pan and fry the spring onions (scallions) until translucent. Remove with a slotted spoon and drain on paper towels. Beat together the Ricotta, yogurt and half the Gruyère. Beat in the egg and stir in the cashew nuts and parsley. Season with salt and cayenne pepper.

3 Lightly brush a small, heavy frying pan with oil and heat. Pour in 3–4 tablespoons of the pancake batter and tilt the pan so that it covers the base. Cook for about 3 minutes, until bubbles appear in the centre. Turn and cook the other side for about 2 minutes, until lightly browned. Slide the pancake on a warmed plate, cover with foil and keep warm while you cook the remainder. It should make 8–12 pancakes.

4 Spread a little filling over each pancake and fold in half and then half again, envelope style. Spoon the remaining filling into the opening.

5 Grease a shallow, ovenproof dish and arrange the pancakes in a single layer. Sprinkle on the remaining cheese and cook in the preheated oven for about 15 minutes. Serve hot, garnished with lemon wedges and coriander (cilantro) sprigs.

Step *3*

Step *4*

Step *5*

Butter-Crust Tartlets with Feta Cheese

These crisp-baked bread cases, filled with sliced tomatoes, Feta cheese,
black olives and quail's eggs, are quick to make and taste delicious.

SERVES 4

INGREDIENTS

8 slices bread from a medium-cut large loaf
125 g/4 oz/½ cup butter, melted
125 g/4 oz Feta cheese, cut into small cubes
4 cherry tomatoes, cut into wedges
8 pitted black or green olives, halved
8 quail's eggs, hard-boiled
2 tbsp olive oil
1 tbsp wine vinegar
1 tsp wholegrain mustard
pinch of caster (superfine) sugar
salt and pepper
fresh parsley sprigs, to garnish

1 Remove the crusts from the bread. Trim the bread into squares and flatten each piece with a rolling pin.

2 Brush the bread with melted butter, and then arrange them in bun or muffin tins. Press a piece of crumpled foil into each bread case to secure in place. Bake in a preheated oven, 190°C/375°F/Gas Mark 5, for about 10 minutes, or until crisp and browned.

3 Meanwhile, mix together the Feta cheese, tomatoes and olives. Shell the eggs and quarter them. Mix together the olive oil, vinegar, mustard and sugar. Season with salt and pepper.

4 Remove the bread cases from the oven and discard the foil. Leave to cool.

5 Just before serving, fill the bread cases with the cheese and tomato mixture. Arrange the eggs on top and spoon over the dressing. Garnish with parsley sprigs.

Step *1*

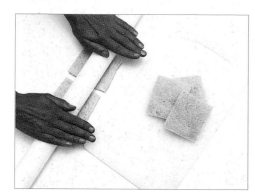

Step *2*

Step *5*

Aubergine (Eggplant) & Mushroom Satay with Peanut Sauce

Grilled, skewered vegetables are served with a satay sauce.

SERVES 4

INGREDIENTS

2 aubergines (eggplants),
cut into 2.5 cm/1 inch pieces
175 g/6 oz small chestnut mushrooms

MARINADE

1 tsp cumin seeds
1 tsp coriander seeds
2.5 cm/1 inch piece ginger root, grated
2 garlic cloves, crushed lightly
½ stalk lemon grass, chopped roughly
4 tbsp light soy sauce
8 tbsp sunflower oil
2 tbsp lemon juice

PEANUT SAUCE

½ tsp cumin seeds
½ tsp coriander seeds
3 garlic cloves
1 small onion, quartered
1 tbsp lemon juice
1 tsp salt
½ red chilli, deseeded and sliced
120 ml/4 fl oz/½ cup coconut milk
250 g/8 oz/1 cup crunchy peanut butter
250 ml/8 fl oz/1 cup water

1 Thread the aubergines (eggplants) and mushrooms on to eight wooden or metal skewers. If using wooden skewers, soak in hand-hot water for 5 minutes.

2 To make the marinade, grind the cumin and coriander seeds, ginger, garlic and lemon grass together. Put in a wok or a large frying pan (skillet). Stir over a high heat until fragrant. Remove from the heat and add the remaining marinade ingredients.

3 Place the skewers in a non-porous dish and spoon the marinade over. Leave to marinate for a minimum of 2 hours and up to 8 hours.

4 To make the peanut sauce, grind together the cumin and coriander seeds and the garlic. Purée the onion in a food processor or blender, or chop finely by hand, then add to the cumin seed mixture. Add the rest of the ingredients in order, except the water.

5 Transfer to a saucepan and blend in the water. Bring to the boil and cook until the required thickness is reached. Transfer to a serving bowl.

6 Place the skewers on a baking sheet and cook under a preheated very hot grill (broiler) for 15–20 minutes. Brush with the marinade frequently and turn once. Serve with the peanut sauce.

Step *2*

Step *3*

Step *5*

Mediterranean Vegetable Tart

A rich tomato pastry base topped with a mouthwatering selection of vegetables and cheese makes a tart that's tasty as well as attractive.

SERVES 6

INGREDIENTS

1 aubergine (eggplant), sliced
2 tbsp salt
4 tbsp olive oil
1 garlic clove, crushed
1 large yellow (bell) pepper, deseeded
and sliced
300 ml/½ pint/1¼ cups ready-made
tomato pasta sauce
125 g/4 oz/⅔ cup sun-dried tomatoes in oil,
drained and halved if necessary
175 g/6 oz Mozzarella,
drained and sliced thinly

PASTRY

250 g/8 oz/2 cups plain (all-purpose) flour
pinch of celery salt
125 g/4 oz/½ cup butter or margarine
2 tbsp tomato purée (paste)
2–3 tbsp milk

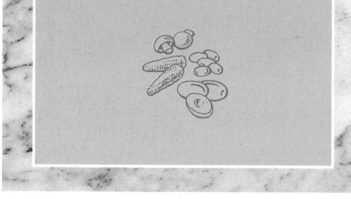

1 To make the pastry, sift the flour and celery salt into a bowl and rub in the butter or margarine until the mixture resembles fine breadcrumbs.

2 Mix together the tomato purée (paste) and milk and stir into the mixture to form a firm dough. Knead gently on a lightly floured surface until smooth. Wrap and chill for 30 minutes.

3 Grease a 28 cm/11 inch loose-bottomed flan tin. Roll out the pastry on a lightly floured surface and use to line the tin. Trim and prick all over with a fork. Chill for 30 minutes.

4 Meanwhile, layer the aubergine (eggplant) in a dish, sprinkling with the salt. Leave for 30 minutes.

5 Bake the pastry case in a preheated oven, 200°C/400°F/Gas Mark 6, for 20–25 minutes until cooked and lightly golden. Set aside. Increase the oven temperature to 230°C/450°F/Gas Mark 8.

6 Rinse the aubergine (eggplant) and pat dry. Heat 3 tablespoons of the oil in a frying pan (skillet) and gently fry the garlic, aubergine (eggplant) and (bell) pepper for 5–6 minutes until just softened. Drain on paper towels.

7 Spread the pastry case with pasta sauce and arrange the cooked vegetables, sun-dried tomatoes and Mozzarella on top. Brush with the remaining oil and bake for 5 minutes until the cheese is just melting.

Step *2*

Step *6*

Step *7*

Baked Aubergine (Eggplant), Basil & Mozzarella Rolls

Thin slices of aubergine (eggplant) are fried in olive oil and garlic, and then topped with pesto sauce and finely sliced Mozzarella.

SERVES 4

INGREDIENTS

2 aubergines (eggplant), sliced thinly lengthways
5 tbsp olive oil
1 garlic clove, crushed
4 tbsp pesto
175 g/6 oz/1½ cups Mozzarella, grated
basil leaves, torn into pieces
salt and pepper
fresh basil leaves, to garnish

1 Sprinkle the aubergine (eggplant) slices liberally with salt and leave for 10–15 minutes to extract the bitter juices. Turn the slices over and repeat. Rinse well with cold water and drain on paper towels.

2 Heat the olive oil in a large frying pan (skillet) and add the garlic. Fry the aubergine (eggplant) slices lightly on both sides, a few at a time. Drain them on paper towels.

3 Spread the pesto on to one side of the aubergine (eggplant) slices. Top with the grated Mozzarella and sprinkle with the torn basil leaves. Season with a little salt and pepper. Roll up the slices and secure with wooden cocktail sticks (toothpicks).

4 Arrange the aubergine (eggplant) rolls in a greased ovenproof baking dish. Place in a preheated oven, 180°C/350°F/Gas Mark 4, and bake for 8–10 minutes.

5 Transfer the rolls to a warmed serving plate. Scatter with fresh basil leaves and serve at once.

Step 2

Step 3

Step 4

Crispy-Fried Vegetables with Hot & Sweet Dipping Sauce

A Thai-style dipping sauce makes the perfect accompaniment to fresh vegetables coated in a light batter and deep-fried.

SERVES 4

INGREDIENTS

vegetable oil for deep-frying
500 g/1 lb selection of vegetables, such as cauliflower, broccoli, mushrooms, courgettes (zucchini), (bell) peppers and baby sweetcorn, cut into even-sized pieces

BATTER

125 g/4 oz/1 cup plain (all-purpose) flour
½ tsp salt
1 tsp caster (superfine) sugar
1 tsp baking powder
3 tbsp vegetable oil
200 ml/7 fl oz/scant 1 cup warm water

SAUCE

6 tbsp light malt vinegar
2 tbsp Thai fish sauce or light soy sauce
2 tbsp water
1 tbsp soft brown sugar
pinch of salt
2 garlic cloves, crushed
2 tsp grated ginger root
2 red chillies, deseeded and chopped finely
2 tbsp chopped fresh coriander (cilantro)

1 To make the batter, sift the flour, salt, sugar and baking powder into a large bowl. Add the oil and most of the water. Whisk together to make a smooth batter, adding extra water to give it the consistency of single cream. Chill for 20–30 minutes.

2 Meanwhile, make the sauce. Heat the vinegar, fish sauce or soy sauce, water, sugar and salt until boiling. Remove from the heat and leave to cool.

3 Mix together the garlic, ginger, chillies and coriander (cilantro) in a small serving bowl. Add the cooled vinegar mixture and stir together.

4 Heat the vegetable oil for deep-frying in a wok or deep–fryer. Dip the prepared vegetables in the batter and fry them, a few at a time, until crisp and golden – about 2 minutes. Drain on paper towels.

5 Serve the vegetables accompanied by the dipping sauce.

Step *2*

Step *3*

Step *4*

Fried Tofu (Bean Curd) with Peanut Sauce

This is a very sociable dish if put in the centre of the table where people can help themselves with cocktail sticks.

SERVES 4

INGREDIENTS

500 g/1 lb marinated or plain tofu (bean curd)
2 tbsp rice vinegar
2 tbsp sugar
1 tsp salt
3 tbsp smooth peanut butter
½ tsp chilli flakes
3 tbsp barbecue sauce
1 litre/1¾ pints/4 cups sunflower oil
2 tbsp sesame oil

BATTER

4 tbsp plain (all-purpose) flour
2 eggs, beaten
4 tbsp milk
½ tsp baking powder
½ tsp chilli powder

1 Cut the tofu (bean curd) into 2.5 cm/1 inch triangles. Set aside.

2 Combine the vinegar, sugar and salt in a saucepan. Bring to the boil and then simmer for 2 minutes. Remove from the heat and add the peanut butter, chilli flakes and barbecue sauce.

3 To make the batter, sift the flour into a bowl, make a well in the centre and add the eggs. Draw in the flour, adding the milk slowly. Stir in the baking powder and chilli powder.

4 Heat both the oils in a deep-fryer or large saucepan until a light haze appears on top.

5 Dip the tofu (bean curd) triangles into the batter and deep-fry until golden brown. Drain on paper towels. Serve with the peanut sauce.

Step *1*

Step *2*

Step *5*

PASTA DISHES

Pasta is one of the most popular and versatile foods on sale today. Available fresh or dried, pasta is made in a wide variety of colours and flavours, shapes and sizes, each lending itself to a particular type of sauce. For instance, flat ribbons go well with cream or cheese-based sauces; tubes and shapes are ideal for trapping chunkier sauces in their crevices. Wholewheat pastas have a chewier texture and are valuable for the additional fibre they contain.

Pasta is a marvellous convenience food - both nourishing and satisfying. All types are quick to cook and provide good basic food that can be dressed up in all kinds of ways. From family favourites such as Three-Cheese Macaroni Bake (page 110) to quick supper dishes such as Spring Vegetables and Tofu Fusilli (page 112), pasta combines very well with vegetables, herbs, nuts and cheeses, to provide scores of interesting and tasty meals.

Tagliatelle Tricolore with Broccoli & Blue Cheese Sauce

Some of the simplest and most satisfying dishes are made with pasta, such as this delicious combination of tagliatelle with its two-cheese sauce.

SERVES 4

INGREDIENTS

300 g/10 oz dried tagliatelle tricolore
(plain, spinach-and tomato-flavoured noodles)
250 g/8 oz/2½ cups broccoli, broken into small florets
350g/12 oz/1½ cups Mascarpone cheese
125 g/4 oz/1 cup blue cheese, chopped
1 tbsp chopped fresh oregano
30 g/1 oz/2 tbsp butter
salt and pepper
sprigs of fresh oregano, to garnish
freshly grated Parmesan, to serve

1 Cook the tagliatelle in plenty of boiling salted water until just tender, according to the instructions on the packet. The Italians call this al dente, which literally means 'to the tooth'.

2 Meanwhile, cook the broccoli florets in a small amount of lightly salted, boiling water. Avoid overcooking the broccoli, so that it retains its colour and texture.

3 Heat the Mascarpone and blue cheeses together gently in a large saucepan until they are melted. Stir in the oregano and season with salt and pepper.

4 Drain the pasta thoroughly. Return it to the saucepan and add the butter, tossing the tagliatelle to coat it. Drain the broccoli well and add to the pasta with the sauce, tossing gently to mix.

5 Divide the pasta between 4 warmed serving plates. Garnish with sprigs of fresh oregano and serve with freshly grated Parmesan.

Step *1*

Step *3*

Step *4*

Pasta with Pine Kernels (Nuts) & Blue Cheese

Simple, quick and inexpensive, this tasty pasta dish can be prepared in minutes.

SERVES 4

INGREDIENTS

60 g/2 oz/1 cup pine kernels (nuts)
350 g/12 oz dried pasta shapes
2 courgettes (zucchini), sliced
125 g/4 oz/1¼ cups broccoli, broken into florets
200 g/7 oz/1 cup full-fat soft cheese
150 ml/½ pint/⅔ cup milk
1 tbsp chopped fresh basil
125 g/4 oz button mushrooms, sliced
90 g/3 oz blue cheese, crumbled
salt and pepper
sprigs of fresh basil, to garnish
green salad, to serve

1 Scatter the pine kernels (nuts) on to a baking sheet (cookie sheet) and grill (broil), turning occasionally, until lightly browned all over. Set aside.

2 Cook the pasta in plenty of boiling salted water for 8–10 minutes until just tender. Meanwhile, cook the courgettes (zucchini) and broccoli in a small amount of boiling, lightly salted water for about 5 minutes until just tender.

3 Put the soft cheese into a saucepan and heat gently, stirring constantly. Add the milk and stir to mix.

4 Add the basil and mushrooms and cook gently for 2–3 minutes. Stir in the blue cheese and season to taste.

5 Drain the pasta and the vegetables and mix together. Pour over the cheese and mushroom sauce and add the pine kernels (nuts). Toss gently to mix. Garnish with basil sprigs and serve with a green salad.

Step *1*   **Step** *3*   **Step** *4*

Three-Cheese Macaroni Bake

Based on a traditional family favourite, this pasta bake has plenty of flavour. Serve with a crisp salad for a quick, tasty supper.

SERVES 4

INGREDIENTS

600 ml/1 pint/2½ cups Béchamel Sauce
(page 12)
250 g/8 oz/2 cups macaroni
1 egg, beaten
125 g/4 oz/1 cup grated mature
(sharp) Cheddar
1 tbsp wholegrain mustard
2 tbsp chopped fresh chives
4 tomatoes, sliced
125 g/4 oz/1 cup grated Red Leicester
(brick) cheese
60 g/2 oz/½ cup grated blue cheese
2 tbsp sunflower seeds
salt and pepper
snipped fresh chives, to garnish

1 Make the béchamel sauce, put into a bowl and cover with clingfilm (plastic wrap) to prevent a skin forming. Set aside.

2 Bring a saucepan of salted water to the boil and cook the macaroni for 8–10 minutes until just tender. Drain well and place in an ovenproof dish.

3 Stir the beaten egg, Cheddar, mustard, chives and seasoning into the béchamel sauce and spoon over the macaroni, making sure it is well covered. Top with a layer of sliced tomatoes.

4 Sprinkle over the Red Leicester (brick) and blue cheeses, and sunflower seeds. Put on a baking sheet (cookie sheet) and bake in a preheated oven, 190°C/375°F/Gas Mark 5, for 25–30 minutes until bubbling and golden. Garnish with chives and serve immediately.

Step *2*

Step *3*

Step *4*

Spring Vegetable & Tofu (Bean Curd) Fusilli

*This is a simple, clean-tasting dish of green vegetables,
tofu (bean curd) and pasta, lightly tossed in olive oil.*

SERVES 4

INGREDIENTS

250 g/8 oz asparagus
125 g/4 oz mangetout (snow peas)
250 g/8 oz French (green) beans
1 leek
250 g/8 oz shelled small broad (fava) beans
300 g/10 oz dried fusilli
2 tbsp olive oil
30 g/1 oz/2 tbsp butter or margarine
1 garlic clove, crushed
250 g/8 oz tofu (bean curd), cut into
2.5 cm/1 inch cubes
60 g/2 oz/⅓ cup pitted green olives in brine,
drained
salt and pepper
freshly grated Parmesan, to serve

1 Cut the asparagus into 5 cm/2 inch lengths. Finely slice the mangetout (snow peas) diagonally and slice the French (green) beans into 2.5 cm/1 inch pieces. Finely slice the leek.

2 Bring a large saucepan of water to the boil and add the asparagus, green beans and broad (fava) beans. Bring back to the boil and cook for 4 minutes until just tender. Drain well and rinse in cold water. Set aside.

3 Bring a large saucepan of salted water to the boil and cook the fusilli for 8–9 minutes until just tender. Drain well. Toss in 1 tablespoon of the oil and season well.

4 Meanwhile, in a wok or large frying pan (skillet), heat the remaining oil and the butter or margarine and gently fry the leek, garlic and tofu (bean curd) for 1–2 minutes until the vegetables have just softened.

5 Stir in the mangetout (snow peas) and cook for a further minute.

6 Add the boiled vegetables and olives to the pan and heat through for 1 minute. Carefully stir in the pasta and seasoning. Cook for 1 minute and pile into a warmed serving dish. Serve sprinkled with Parmesan.

Step *1*

Step *4*

Step *6*

Pasta Provençale

A Mediterranean mixture of red (bell) peppers, garlic and courgettes (zucchini) cooked in olive oil and tossed with pasta.

SERVES 4

INGREDIENTS

3 tbsp olive oil
1 onion, sliced
2 garlic cloves, chopped
3 red (bell) peppers,
deseeded and cut into strips
3 courgettes (zucchini), sliced
425 g/14 oz can chopped tomatoes
3 tbsp sun-dried tomato paste
2 tbsp chopped fresh basil
250 g/8 oz fresh pasta spirals
125 g/4 oz/1 cup grated Gruyère cheese
salt and pepper
fresh basil sprigs, to garnish

1 Heat the oil in a heavy-based saucepan or flameproof casserole. Add the onion and garlic and cook, stirring occasionally, until softened. Add the (bell) peppers and courgettes (zucchini) and fry for 5 minutes, stirring occasionally.

2 Add the tomatoes, sun-dried tomato paste, basil and seasoning. Cover and cook for a further 5 minutes.

3 Meanwhile, bring a large saucepan of salted water to the boil and add the pasta. Stir and bring back to the boil. Reduce the heat slightly and cook, uncovered, for 3 minutes, until just tender. Drain thoroughly and add to the vegetables. Toss gently to mix well.

4 Put the mixture into a shallow ovenproof dish and sprinkle over the cheese.

5 Cook under a preheated grill (broiler) for 5 minutes until the cheese is golden brown. Garnish with basil sprigs and serve.

Step *1*

Step *3*

Step *4*

Thai-Style Stir-Fried Noodles

*This dish is considered the Thai national dish, as it is made and eaten
everywhere – a one-dish fast food for eating on the move.*

SERVES 4

INGREDIENTS

250 g/8 oz dried rice noodles
2 red chillies, deseeded and chopped finely
2 shallots, chopped finely
2 tbsp sugar
2 tbsp tamarind water
1 tbsp lime juice
2 tbsp light soy sauce
black pepper
1 tbsp sunflower oil
1 tsp sesame oil
175 g/6 oz/¾ cup smoked tofu (bean curd), diced
2 tbsp chopped roasted peanuts, to garnish

1 Cook the rice noodles as directed on the pack, or soak them in boiling water for 5 minutes.

2 Grind together the chillies, shallots, sugar, tamarind water, lime juice, light soy sauce and black pepper.

3 Heat both the oils together in a wok or large, heavy frying pan (skillet) over a high heat. Add the tofu (bean curd) and stir for 1 minute.

4 Add the chilli mixture, bring to the boil, and stir for about 2 minutes until thickened.

5 Drain the rice noodles and add them to the chilli mixture. Use 2 spoons to lift and stir them until they are no longer steaming. Serve immediately, garnished with the peanuts.

Step *2*

Step *4*

Step *5*

Fried Noodles with Bean-Sprouts, Chives & Chillies

This is a simple idea to jazz up noodles which accompany main course dishes in Thailand.

SERVES 4

INGREDIENTS

500 g/1 lb medium egg noodles
60 g/2 oz/1 cup bean-sprouts
15 g/½ oz chives
3 tbsp sunflower oil
1 garlic clove, crushed
4 green chillies, deseeded,
sliced and soaked in 2 tbsp rice vinegar
salt

1 To cook the noodles, soak in boiling water for 10 minutes. Drain and set aside.

2 Soak the bean-sprouts in cold water while you cut the chives into 2.5 cm/1 inch pieces. Set a few chives aside for garnish. Drain the bean-sprouts thoroughly.

3 Heat the oil in a wok or large, heavy frying pan (skillet). Add the crushed garlic and stir; then add the chillies and stir until fragrant, about 1 minute.

4 Add the bean-sprouts, stir and then add the noodles. Stir in some salt and the chives. Using 2 spoons, lift and stir the noodles for 1 minute.

5 Garnish the finished dish with the reserved chives, and serve immediately.

Step *1*

Step *3*

·Step *4*

GRAINS & PULSES (LEGUMES)

Grains are the seeds of cultivated grasses, while pulses (legumes) are the dried seeds of the pod-bearing plants of the Leguminosae family. Together they are the most universally important staple foods. Grains include wheat, corn, barley, rye, oats, buckwheat and many varieties of rice, as well as associated flours. Pulses (legumes) include chick-peas (garbanzo beans), yellow and green split peas, a fascinating variety of beans together with many types of lentil.

Grains and pulses (legumes) form a substantial base to which other ingredients can be added. Each has its own distinctive flavour and texture, so it's worth experimenting with less well-known varieties. An excellent source of protein, iron, calcium and B vitamins, these valuable foods are cheap, highly nutritious, versatile and filling, and are virtually fat-free. With the current emphasis on healthier eating, they are a must for the modern diet.

Oriental-Style Millet Pilau

Millet makes an interesting alternative to rice, which is the more traditional ingredient for a pilau. Serve with a crisp salad of oriental vegetables.

SERVES 4

INGREDIENTS

300 g/10 oz/1½ cups millet grains
1 tbsp vegetable oil
1 bunch spring onions (scallions),
white and green parts, chopped
1 garlic clove, crushed
1 tsp grated ginger root
1 orange (bell) pepper, deseeded and diced
600 ml/1 pint/2½ cups water
1 orange
125 g/4 oz/⅔ cup chopped pitted dates
2 tsp sesame oil
125 g/4 oz/1 cup roasted cashew nuts
2 tbsp pumpkin seeds
salt and pepper
oriental salad vegetables, to serve

1 Place the millet in a large saucepan and put over a medium heat for 4–5 minutes to toast, shaking the pan occasionally until the grains begin to crack and pop.

2 Heat the oil in another saucepan and gently fry the spring onions (scallions), garlic, ginger and (bell) pepper for 2–3 minutes until just softened but not browned. Add the millet and pour in the water.

3 Using a vegetable peeler, pare the rind from the orange and add the rind to the pan. Squeeze the juice from the orange into the pan. Season well.

4 Bring to the boil, reduce the heat, cover and cook gently for 20 minutes until all the liquid has been absorbed. Remove from the heat, stir in the dates and sesame oil and leave to stand for 10 minutes.

5 Discard the orange rind and stir in the cashew nuts. Pile into a serving dish, sprinkle with pumpkin seeds and serve with oriental salad vegetables.

Step *1*

Step *3*

Step *4*

Chick-Pea (Garbanzo Beans) & Peanut Balls with Hot Chilli Sauce

These tasty, nutty morsels are delicious served with a fiery, tangy sauce that counteracts the richness of the peanuts.

SERVES 4

INGREDIENTS

3 tbsp groundnut oil
1 onion, chopped finely
1 celery stalk, chopped
1 tsp dried mixed herbs
250 g/8 oz/2 cups roasted unsalted peanuts, ground
175 g/6 oz/1 cup canned chick-peas
(garbanzo beans), drained and mashed
1 tsp yeast extract
60 g/2 oz/1 cup fresh wholemeal (whole wheat)
breadcrumbs
1 egg yolk
30 g/1 oz/¼ cup plain (all-purpose) flour
strips of fresh red chilli, to garnish

HOT CHILLI SAUCE

2 tsp groundnut oil
1 large red chilli, deseeded and chopped finely
2 spring onions (scallions), chopped finely
2 tbsp red wine vinegar
200 g/7 oz can chopped tomatoes
2 tbsp tomato purée (paste)
2 tsp caster (superfine) sugar
salt and pepper

TO SERVE

rice
green salad

1 Heat 1 tablespoon of the oil in a frying pan (skillet) and gently fry the onion and celery for 3–4 minutes until softened but not browned.

2 Place all the other ingredients, except the remaining oil and the flour, in a mixing bowl and add the onion and celery. Mix well.

3 Divide the mixture into twelve portions and roll into small balls. Coat with the flour.

4 Heat the remaining oil in a frying pan (skillet). Add the chick-pea (garbanzo bean) balls and cook over a medium heat for 15 minutes, turning frequently, until cooked through and golden. Drain on paper towels.

5 Meanwhile, make the hot chilli sauce. Heat the oil in a small frying pan (skillet) and gently fry the chilli and spring onions (scallions) for 2–3 minutes. Stir in the remaining ingredients and season. Bring to the boil and simmer for 5 minutes.

6 Serve the chick-pea (garbanzo bean) and peanut balls with the hot chilli sauce, rice and a green salad.

 Step *2*

 Step *3*

 Step *4*

Indonesian Hot Rice Salad

*Nutty brown rice combines well with peanuts and a sweet and sour mixture
of fruit and vegetables in this tangy combination.*

SERVES 4

INGREDIENTS

300 g/10 oz/1½ cups brown rice
425 g/14 oz can pineapple pieces
in natural juice, drained
1 bunch spring onions (scallions), chopped
1 red (bell) pepper, deseeded and chopped
125 g/4 oz/2 cups bean-sprouts
90 g/3 oz/¾ cup dry-roasted peanuts
125 g/4 oz radishes, sliced thinly

DRESSING

2 tbsp crunchy peanut butter
1 tbsp groundnut oil
2 tbsp light soy sauce
2 tbsp white wine vinegar
2 tsp clear honey
1 tsp chilli powder
½ tsp garlic salt
pepper

1 Put the rice in a saucepan and cover with water. Bring to the boil, then cover and simmer for 30 minutes until tender.

2 Meanwhile, make the dressing. Place all the ingredients in a small bowl and whisk for a few seconds until well combined.

3 Drain the rice and place in a heatproof bowl. Heat the dressing in a small saucepan for 1 minute and then toss into the rice and mix well.

4 Working quickly, stir in the pineapple, spring onions (scallions), (bell) pepper, bean-sprouts and peanuts.

5 Pile into a warmed serving dish, arrange the radish slices around the outside and serve immediately.

Step *2*

Step *3*

Step *4*

Mushroom & Parmesan Risotto

Make this creamy risotto with Italian arborio rice and freshly grated Parmesan for the best results.

SERVES 4

INGREDIENTS

2 tbsp olive or vegetable oil
250 g/8 oz/generous 1 cup arborio (risotto) rice
2 garlic cloves, crushed
1 onion, chopped
2 celery stalks, chopped
1 red or green (bell) pepper,
deseeded and chopped
250 g/8 oz mushrooms, sliced
1 tbsp chopped fresh oregano
or 1 tsp dried oregano
1 litre/1¾ pints/4 cups Fresh Vegetable
Stock (page 12)
60 g/2 oz sun-dried tomatoes in olive oil,
drained and chopped (optional)
60 g/2 oz/½ cup freshly grated Parmesan
salt and pepper

TO GARNISH

fresh flat-leaf parsley sprigs
fresh bay leaves

1 Heat the oil in a wok or large frying pan (skillet). Add the rice and cook, stirring, for 5 minutes.

2 Add the garlic, onion, celery and (bell) pepper and cook, stirring, for 5 minutes. Add the mushrooms and cook for a further 3–4 minutes.

3 Stir in the oregano and stock. Heat until just boiling, then reduce the heat, cover and simmer gently for about 20 minutes until the rice is tender and creamy.

4 Add the sun-dried tomatoes, if using, and season to taste. Stir in half the Parmesan. Top with the remaining cheese, and garnish with flat-leaf parsley and bay leaves.

Step *1*

Step *3*

Step *4*

Cheesy Semolina Fritters with Apple Relish

Based on a gnocchi recipe, these delicious fritters are accompanied by a fruity home-made relish.

SERVES 4

INGREDIENTS

600 ml/1 pint/2½ cups milk
1 small onion
1 celery stalk
1 bay leaf
2 cloves
125 g/4 oz/⅔ cup semolina
125 g/4 oz/1 cup grated mature (sharp) Cheddar
½ tsp dried mustard powder
2 tbsp plain (all-purpose) flour
1 egg, beaten
60 g/2 oz/½ cup dried white breadcrumbs
6 tbsp vegetable oil
salt and pepper
celery leaves to garnish
coleslaw, to serve

RELISH

2 celery stalks, chopped
2 small dessert (eating) apples, cored and diced finely
90 g/3 oz/½ cup sultanas (golden raisins)
90 g/3 oz/½ cup no-soak dried apricots, chopped
6 tbsp cider vinegar
pinch of ground cloves
½ tsp ground cinnamon

1 Pour the milk into a saucepan and add the onion, celery, bay leaf and cloves. Bring to the boil, remove from the heat and allow to stand for 15 minutes.

2 Strain into another saucepan, bring to the boil and sprinkle in the semolina, stirring constantly. Reduce the heat and simmer for 5 minutes until very thick, stirring occasionally to prevent it sticking.

3 Remove the pan from the heat and beat in the cheese, mustard and seasoning. Place in a greased bowl and allow to cool.

4 To make the relish, put all the ingredients in a saucepan, bring to the boil, cover and simmer gently for 20 minutes, until tender. Allow to cool.

5 Put the flour, egg and breadcrumbs on separate plates. Divide the cooled semolina mixture into eight and press into 6 cm/2½ inch rounds, flouring the hands if necessary.

6 Coat lightly in flour, then egg and breadcrumbs. Heat the oil in a large frying pan (skillet) and gently fry the fritters for 3–4 minutes on each side until golden. Drain on paper towels. Garnish with celery leaves and serve with the relish and coleslaw.

 Step *2*

 Step *5*

Step *6*

Deep South Spiced Rice & Beans

Cajun spices add a flavour of the American deep south to this colourful rice and red kidney bean salad.

SERVES 4

INGREDIENTS

175 g/6 oz/scant 1 cup long-grain rice
4 tbsp olive oil
1 small green (bell) pepper, cored, deseeded and chopped
1 small red (bell) pepper, cored, deseeded and chopped
1 onion, chopped finely
1 small red or green chilli, deseeded and chopped finely
2 tomatoes, chopped
125 g/4 oz/½ cup canned red kidney beans, rinsed and drained
1 tbsp chopped fresh basil
2 tsp chopped fresh thyme (or 1 tsp dried)
1 tsp Cajun spice
salt and pepper
fresh basil leaves, to garnish

1 Cook the rice in plenty of boiling, lightly salted water until just tender, about 12 minutes. Rinse with cold water and drain well.

2 Meanwhile, heat the olive oil in a frying pan (skillet) and fry the green and red (bell) peppers and onion together gently until softened, about 5 minutes.

3 Add the chilli and tomatoes, and cook for a further 2 minutes.

4 Add the vegetable mixture and red kidney beans to the rice. Stir well to combine thoroughly.

5 Stir the chopped herbs and Cajun spice into the rice mixture. Season well with salt and pepper, and serve, garnished with basil leaves.

Step *2*

Step *4*

Step *5*

Egg & Chick-Pea (Garbanzo Bean) Curry

This easy vegetarian curry is always enjoyed. Double the quantities for a great dish if you're cooking for a crowd.

SERVES 4

INGREDIENTS

2 tbsp vegetable oil
2 garlic cloves, crushed
1 large onion, chopped
1 large carrot, sliced
1 apple, cored and chopped
2 tbsp medium-hot curry powder
1 tsp finely grated ginger root
2 tsp paprika
900 ml/1½ pints/3½ cups Fresh Vegetable Stock (page 12)
2 tbsp tomato purée (paste)
½ small cauliflower, broken into florets
475 g/15 oz can chick-peas (garbanzo beans), rinsed and drained
30 g/1 oz/2 tbsp sultanas (golden raisins) or raisins
2 tbsp cornflour (cornstarch)
2 tbsp water
4 hard-boiled (hard-cooked) eggs, quartered
salt and pepper
paprika, to garnish

CUCUMBER DIP

7.5 cm/3 inch piece cucumber, chopped finely
1 tbsp chopped fresh mint
150 ml/¼ pint/⅔ cup natural yogurt
sprigs of fresh mint, to garnish

1 Heat the oil in a large saucepan and fry the garlic, onion, carrot and apple for 4–5 minutes, until softened.

2 Add the curry powder, ginger and paprika and fry for 1 minute more.

3 Stir in the vegetable stock and tomato purée (paste).

4 Add the cauliflower, chick-peas (garbanzo beans) and sultanas (golden raisins) or raisins. Bring to the boil, then reduce the heat and simmer, covered, for 25–30 minutes until the vegetables are tender.

5 Blend the cornflour (cornstarch) with the water and add to the curry, stirring until thickened. Cook gently for 2 minutes. Season to taste.

6 To make the dip, mix together the cucumber, mint and yogurt in a small serving bowl.

7 Ladle the curry on to four warmed serving plates and arrange the eggs on top. Sprinkle with a little paprika. Garnish the cucumber and mint dip with mint and serve with the curry.

Step 2

Step 3

Step 4

Pesto Rice with Garlic Bread

**Try this combination of two types of rice with the richness of pine kernels
(nuts), basil, and freshly grated Parmesan.**

SERVES 4

INGREDIENTS

300 g/10 oz/1½ cups mixed long-grain
and wild rice
fresh basil sprigs, to garnish
tomato and orange salad, to serve

PESTO DRESSING

15 g/½ oz fresh basil
125 g/4 oz/1 cup pine kernels (nuts)
2 garlic cloves, crushed
6 tbsp olive oil
60 g/2 oz/½ cup freshly grated Parmesan
salt and pepper

GARLIC BREAD

2 small granary or whole wheat
French bread sticks
90 g/3 oz/½ cup butter or margarine, softened
2 garlic cloves, crushed
1 tsp dried mixed herbs

1 Place the rice in a saucepan and cover with water. Bring to the boil and cook according to the packet instructions. Drain well and keep warm.

2 Meanwhile, make the pesto dressing. Remove the basil leaves from the stalks and finely chop the leaves. Reserve 30 g/1 oz/¼ cup of the pine kernels (nuts) and finely chop the remainder. Mix with the chopped basil and dressing ingredients. Alternatively, put all the ingredients in a food processor or blender and blend for a few seconds until smooth. Set aside.

3 To make the garlic bread, slice the bread at 2.5 cm/1 inch intervals, taking care not to slice all the way through. Mix the butter or margarine with the garlic, herbs and seasoning. Spread thickly between each slice.

4 Wrap the bread in foil and bake in a preheated oven, 200°C/400°F/Gas Mark 6, for 10–15 minutes.

5 To serve, toast the reserved pine kernels (nuts) under a preheated medium grill (broiler) for 2–3 minutes until golden. Toss the pesto dressing into the hot rice and pile into a warmed serving dish. Sprinkle with toasted pine kernels (nuts) and garnish with basil sprigs. Serve with the garlic bread and a tomato and orange salad.

Step *2*

Step *3*

Step *5*

Chatuchak Fried Rice

An excellent way to use up leftover rice. Pop it in the freezer as soon as it is cool, and it will be ready to reheat at any time.

SERVES 4

INGREDIENTS

1 tbsp sunflower oil
3 shallots, chopped finely
2 garlic cloves, crushed
1 red chilli, deseeded and chopped finely
2.5 cm/1 inch piece ginger root, shredded finely
½ green (bell) pepper, deseeded and
sliced finely
150 g/5 oz/2–3 baby aubergines
(eggplants), quartered
90 g/3 oz sugar snap peas or mangetout
(snow peas), trimmed and blanched
90 g/3 oz/6 baby sweetcorn, halved lengthways
and blanched
1 tomato, cut into 8 pieces
90 g/3 oz/1½ cups bean-sprouts
500 g/1 lb/3 cups cooked Thai jasmine rice
2 tbsp tomato ketchup
2 tbsp light soy sauce

TO GARNISH

fresh coriander (cilantro) leaves
lime wedges

1 Heat the oil in a wok or large, heavy frying pan (skillet) over a high heat. Add the shallots, garlic, chilli and ginger. Stir until the shallots have softened.

2 Add the green (bell) pepper and baby aubergines (eggplants) and stir. Add the sugar snap peas or mangetout (snow peas), baby sweetcorn, tomato and bean-sprouts. Stir for 3 minutes.

3 Add the rice, and lift and stir with two spoons for 4–5 minutes, until no more steam is released. Stir in the tomato ketchup and soy sauce.

4 Serve immediately, garnished with coriander (cilantro) leaves and lime wedges to squeeze over.

Step *1*

Step *2*

Step *3*

Couscous Royale

Serve this stunning dish as a centrepiece for a Moroccan-style feast;
a truly memorable meal.

SERVES 6

INGREDIENTS

3 carrots
3 courgettes (zucchini)
350 g/12 oz pumpkin or squash
1.25 litres/2¼ pints/5 cups Fresh Vegetable
Stock (page 12)
2 cinnamon sticks, broken in half
2 tsp ground cumin
1 tsp ground coriander
pinch of saffron strands
2 tbsp olive oil
pared rind and juice of 1 lemon
2 tbsp clear honey
500 g/1 lb/2⅔ cups pre-cooked couscous
60 g/2 oz/¼ cup butter or margarine, softened
175 g/6 oz/1 cup large seedless raisins
salt and pepper
fresh coriander (cilantro), to garnish

1 Cut the carrots and courgettes (zucchini) into 7 cm/3 inch pieces and cut in half lengthways.

2 Trim the pumpkin or squash and discard the seeds. Peel and cut into pieces the same size as the carrots and courgettes (zucchini).

3 Put the stock, spices, saffron and carrots in a large saucepan. Bring to the boil, skim off any scum and add the olive oil. Simmer for 15 minutes.

4 Add the lemon rind and juice to the pan with the honey, courgettes (zucchini) and pumpkin or squash. Season well. Bring back to the boil and simmer for a further 10 minutes.

5 Meanwhile, soak the couscous according to the packet instructions. Transfer to a steamer or large sieve (strainer) lined with muslin (cheesecloth) and place over the vegetable pan. Cover and steam as directed. Stir in the butter or margarine.

6 Pile the couscous on to a warmed serving plate. Drain the vegetables, reserving the stock, lemon rind and cinnamon. Arrange the vegetables on top of the couscous. Put the raisins on top and spoon over 6 tablespoons of the reserved stock. Keep warm.

7 Return the remaining stock to the heat and boil for 5 minutes to reduce slightly. Discard the lemon rind and cinnamon. Garnish with the coriander (cilantro) and serve with the sauce handed separately.

Step *2*

Step *4*

Step *5*

Kofta Kebabs with Tabbouleh

Traditionally, koftas are made from a spicy meat mixture, but this bean and wheat version makes a tasty alternative.

SERVES 4

INGREDIENTS

175 g/6 oz/1 cup aduki beans
175 g/6 oz/1 cup bulgur wheat
450 ml/¾ pint/scant 2 cups Fresh Vegetable
Stock (page 12)
3 tbsp olive oil
1 onion, chopped finely
2 garlic cloves, crushed
1 tsp ground coriander
1 tsp ground cumin
2 tbsp chopped fresh coriander (cilantro)
3 eggs, beaten
125 g/4 oz/1 cup dried breadcrumbs
salt and pepper

TABBOULEH

175 g/6 oz/1 cup bulgur wheat
2 tbsp lemon juice
1 tbsp olive oil
6 tbsp chopped fresh parsley
4 spring onions (scallions), chopped finely
60 g/2 oz cucumber, chopped finely
3 tbsp chopped fresh mint
1 extra-large tomato, chopped finely

TO SERVE

Tahini Cream (page 12)
black olives
pitta bread

1 Cook the aduki beans in boiling water for 40 minutes until tender. Drain, rinse and leave to cool. Cook the bulgur wheat in the stock for 10 minutes until the stock is absorbed. Set aside.

2 Heat 1 tablespoon of the oil in a frying pan (skillet) and fry the onion, garlic and spices for 4–5 minutes.

3 Transfer to a bowl with the beans, coriander (cilantro), seasoning and eggs and mash with a potato masher or fork. Add the breadcrumbs and bulgur wheat and stir well. Cover and chill for 1 hour, until firm.

4 To make the tabbouleh, soak the bulgar wheat in 450 ml/¾ pint/scant 2 cups of boiling water for 15 minutes. Combine with the remaining ingredients. Cover and chill.

5 With wet hands, mould the kofta mixture into 32 oval shapes.

6 Press on to skewers, brush with oil and grill (broil) for 5–6 minutes until golden. Turn, re-brush, and cook for 5–6 minutes. Drain on paper towels. Garnish and serve with the tabbouleh, tahini cream, black olives and pitta bread.

 Step *3*

 Step *5*

Step *6*

Fried Rice in Pineapple

This has a mild, pleasant flavour and looks very impressive as part of a party buffet, so everyone can enjoy it.

SERVES 4–6

INGREDIENTS

1 large pineapple
1 tbsp sunflower oil
1 garlic clove, crushed
1 small onion, diced
½ celery stalk, sliced
1 tsp coriander seeds, ground
1 tsp cumin seeds, ground
150 g/5 oz/1½ cups button mushrooms, sliced
250 g/8 oz/1⅓ cups cooked rice
2 tbsp light soy sauce
½ tsp sugar
½ tsp salt
30 g/1 oz/¼ cup cashew nuts

TO GARNISH

1 spring onion (scallion), sliced finely
fresh coriander (cilantro) leaves
mint sprig

1 Halve the pineapple lengthways and cut out the flesh to make 2 boat-shaped shells. Cut the flesh into cubes and reserve 125 g/4 oz/1 cup to use in this recipe. (Any remaining pineapple cubes can be served separately.)

2 Heat the oil in a wok or large, heavy frying pan (skillet). Cook the garlic, onion and celery over a high heat, stirring constantly, for 2 minutes. Stir in the coriander and cumin seeds, and the mushrooms.

3 Add the pineapple cubes and cooked rice to the pan and stir well. Stir in the soy sauce, sugar, salt and cashew nuts.

4 Using two spoons, lift and stir the rice for about 4 minutes until it is thoroughly heated.

5 Spoon the rice mixture into the pineapple boats. Garnish with spring onion (scallion), coriander (cilantro) leaves and mint.

Step 2

Step 3

Step 4

Vegetable Curry

Vegetables are cooked in a mildly spiced curry sauce with yogurt and fresh coriander (cilantro) stirred in just before serving.

SERVES 4

INGREDIENTS

2 tbsp sunflower oil
1 onion, sliced
2 tsp cumin seeds
2 tbsp ground coriander
1 tsp ground turmeric
2 tsp ground ginger
1 tsp chopped fresh red chilli
2 garlic cloves, chopped
425 g/14 oz can chopped tomatoes
3 tbsp powdered coconut mixed with
300 ml/½ pint/1¼ cups boiling water
1 small cauliflower, broken into florets
2 courgettes (zucchini), sliced
2 carrots, sliced
1 potato, diced
425 g/14 oz can chick-peas (garbanzo beans),
drained and rinsed
150 ml/¼ pint/¾ cup thick natural yogurt
2 tbsp mango chutney
3 tbsp chopped fresh coriander (cilantro)
salt and pepper
fresh coriander (cilantro) sprigs, to garnish

TO SERVE

onion relish
Raita (page 188)
basmati rice
naan bread

1 Heat the oil in a saucepan and fry the onion until softened. Add the cumin, ground coriander, turmeric, ginger, chilli and garlic and fry for 1 minute.

2 Add the tomatoes and coconut mixture and mix well.

3 Add the cauliflower, courgettes (zucchini), carrots, potato, chick-peas (garbanzo beans) and seasoning. Cover and simmer for 20 minutes until the vegetables are tender.

4 Stir in the yogurt, mango chutney and fresh coriander (cilantro) and heat through gently, but do not boil. Garnish with coriander (cilantro) sprigs and serve with onion relish, raita, basmati rice and naan bread.

Step *1*

Step *3*

Step *4*

Moroccan Vegetable Couscous

*Couscous is a semolina grain which is very quick to cook,
and it makes a pleasant change from rice or pasta.*

SERVES 4

INGREDIENTS

2 tbsp vegetable oil
1 large onion, chopped coarsely
1 carrot, chopped
1 turnip, chopped
600 ml/1 pint/2½ cups Fresh Vegetable
Stock (page 12)
175 g/6 oz/1 cup couscous
2 tomatoes, peeled and quartered
2 courgettes (zucchini), chopped
1 red (bell) pepper, deseeded and chopped
125 g/4 oz French (green) beans, chopped
grated rind of 1 lemon
pinch of ground turmeric (optional)
1 tbsp finely chopped fresh coriander (cilantro)
or parsley
salt and pepper
fresh flat-leaf parsley sprigs, to garnish

1 Heat the oil in a large saucepan and fry the onion, carrot and turnip for 3–4 minutes. Add the vegetable stock and bring to the boil. Cover and simmer gently for about 20 minutes.

2 Meanwhile, put the couscous in a bowl and moisten with a little boiling water, stirring, until the grains have swollen and separated.

3 Add the tomatoes, courgettes (zucchini), (bell) pepper and French (green) beans to the saucepan.

4 Stir the lemon rind and turmeric, if using, into the couscous and mix well. Put the couscous in a steamer and position over the vegetables. Simmer the vegetables so that the couscous steams for 8–10 minutes.

5 Pile the couscous onto warmed serving plates. Ladle the vegetables and some of the liquid over the top. Scatter with the coriander (cilantro) or parsley and serve at once, garnished with parsley sprigs.

Step *1*

Step *2*

Step *3*

STIR-FRIES
& SAUTÉS

*Whether you're cooking a Chinese-style meal or
any other kind of dish, stir-frying is one of the most
convenient and nutritious ways of cooking vegetarian
food. The food is cooked quickly over very high heat in
a very little oil. The high heat seals in the natural juices
and helps preserve nutrients. The short cooking time
makes the vegetables more succulent and preserves
texture as well as the natural flavour and colour.
A round-bottomed wok is ideal for stir-frying as it
conducts and retains heat evenly. The conical shape
requires far less oil than a flat-bottomed frying pan
(skillet), and the food always returns to the centre where
the heat is most intense, however vigorously you stir.
Sautéeing, or shallow-frying, requires a flat-bottomed
pan so that the food can be tossed and stirred without
being too crowded. A brisk heat is essential so that
the food turns golden brown and crisp. If you
use a non-stick pan you can cut down on the
amount of oil required.*

Sauté of Summer Vegetables with Tarragon Dressing

The freshness of lightly cooked summer vegetables is enhanced by the aromatic flavour of a tarragon and white wine dressing.

SERVES 4

INGREDIENTS

250 g/8 oz baby carrots, scrubbed
125 g/4 oz runner (green) beans
2 courgettes (zucchini), trimmed
1 bunch large spring onions (scallions), trimmed
1 bunch radishes, trimmed
60 g/2 oz/¹⁄₂ cup butter
2 tbsp light olive oil
2 tbsp white wine vinegar
4 tbsp dry white wine
1 tsp caster (superfine) sugar
1 tbsp chopped fresh tarragon
salt and pepper
sprigs of fresh tarragon, to garnish

1 Trim and halve the carrots, slice the beans and courgettes (zucchini), and halve the spring onions (scallions) and radishes, so that all the vegetables are cut to even-sized pieces.

2 Melt the butter in a large frying pan (skillet) or wok. Add all the vegetables and fry them over a medium heat, stirring frequently.

3 Heat the olive oil, vinegar, white wine and sugar in a small saucepan. Remove from the heat and add the tarragon.

4 When the vegetables are just cooked, but still retain their crunchiness, pour over the 'dressing'. Stir through, and then transfer to a warmed serving dish. Garnish with sprigs of fresh tarragon and serve at once.

 Step *1*

 Step *2*

Step *4*

Sauté of Summer Vegetables with Tarragon Dressing

Golden Cheese & Leek Potato Cakes

Make these tasty potato cakes for a quick and simple supper dish.
Serve them with scrambled eggs if you're very hungry.

SERVES 4

INGREDIENTS

1 kg/2 lb potatoes
4 tbsp milk
60 g/2 oz/¼ cup butter or margarine
2 leeks, chopped finely
1 onion, chopped finely
175 g/6 oz/1½ cups grated mature
(sharp) Cheddar
1 tbsp chopped fresh parsley or chives
1 egg, beaten
2 tbsp water
90 g/3 oz/1½ cups fresh white
or brown breadcrumbs
vegetable oil for shallow frying
salt and pepper
fresh flat-leaf parsley sprigs, to garnish
mixed salad (greens), to serve

1 Cook the potatoes in lightly salted boiling water until tender. Drain and mash them with the milk and the butter or margarine.

2 Cook the leeks and onion in a small amount of salted boiling water for about 10 minutes until tender. Drain.

3 In a large mixing bowl, combine the leeks and onion with the mashed potato, cheese and parsley or chives. Season to taste.

4 Beat together the egg and water in a shallow bowl. Sprinkle the breadcrumbs into a separate shallow bowl. Shape the potato mixture into 12 even-sized cakes, brushing each with the egg mixture, then coating with the breadcrumbs.

5 Heat the oil in a large frying pan (skillet) and fry the potato cakes gently for about 2–3 minutes on each side until light golden brown. Garnish with flat-leaf parsley and serve with a mixed salad (greens).

Step *1*

Step *4*

Step *5*

Stir-Fried Greens

*This is an easy recipe to make as a quick accompaniment to a main course.
The water chestnuts give a delicious crunch to the greens.*

SERVES 4

INGREDIENTS

1 tbsp sunflower oil
1 garlic clove, halved
2 spring onions (scallions),
sliced finely
200 g/7 oz can water chestnuts,
drained and sliced finely (optional)
500 g/1 lb spinach, tough stalks removed
1 tsp sherry vinegar
1 tsp light soy sauce
pepper

1 Heat the oil in a wok or large, heavy frying pan (skillet) over a high heat.

2 Add the garlic and cook, stirring, for 1 minute. Be careful not to let it burn.

3 Add the spring onions (scallions) and water chestnuts, if using, and stir for 2–3 minutes. Stir in the spinach.

4 Add the sherry vinegar, soy sauce and a sprinkling of pepper. Cook, stirring, until the spinach is tender. Remove the garlic.

5 Transfer to a warmed serving dish, using a slotted spoon in order to drain off the excess liquid. Serve immediately.

Step *3*

Step *4*

Step *5*

Sweetcorn & Potato Fritters

An ideal supper dish for two, or for one if you halve the quantities. You can use the remaining sweetcorn in another recipe.

SERVES 2

INGREDIENTS:

2 tbsp oil
1 small onion, sliced thinly
1 garlic clove, crushed
350 g/12 oz potatoes
200 g/7 oz can sweetcorn, drained
½ tsp dried oregano
1 egg, beaten
60 g/2 oz/½ cup Edam or Gouda cheese, grated
salt and pepper
2–4 eggs
2–4 tomatoes, sliced
parsley sprigs, to garnish

1 Heat 1 tablespoon of the oil in a non-stick frying pan (skillet). Add the onion and garlic, and fry very gently until soft, but only lightly coloured, stirring frequently. Remove from the heat.

2 Grate the potatoes coarsely into a bowl and mix in the sweetcorn, oregano, beaten egg and seasoning; then add the fried onion.

3 Heat the remaining oil in the frying pan (skillet). Divide the potato mixture in half and add to the pan to make two oval-shaped cakes, levelling and shaping the cakes with a palette knife (spatula).

4 Cook gently for about 10 minutes until browned underneath and almost cooked through, keeping in shape with the palette knife (spatula) and loosening so they don't stick.

5 Sprinkle each potato fritter with the grated cheese and place under a preheated moderately hot grill (broiler) until golden brown.

6 Meanwhile, poach either one or two eggs for each person until just cooked. Transfer the fritters to warmed plates and top each with the eggs and sliced tomatoes. Garnish with parsley and serve at once.

Step *2*

Step *3*

Step *5*

Red Curry with Cashews

This is a wonderfully quick dish to prepare. If you don't have time to prepare the curry paste, it can be bought ready-made.

SERVES 4

INGREDIENTS

3 tbsp Red Curry Paste
250 ml/8 fl oz/1 cup coconut milk
1 kaffir lime leaf, mid-rib removed
¼ tsp light soy sauce
60 g/2 oz/4 baby sweetcorn, halved lengthways
125 g/4 oz/1¼ cups broccoli florets
125 g/4 oz French (green) beans,
cut into 5 cm/2 inch pieces
30 g/1 oz/¼ cup cashew nuts
15 fresh basil leaves
1 tbsp chopped fresh coriander (cilantro)
rice, to serve
1 tbsp chopped roast peanuts, to garnish

RED CURRY PASTE

7 fresh red chillies, halved,
deseeded and blanched
(use dried if fresh are not available)
2 tsp cumin seeds
2 tsp coriander seeds
2.5 cm/1 inch piece galangal,
peeled and chopped
½ stalk lemon grass, chopped
1 tsp salt
grated rind of 1 lime
4 garlic cloves, chopped
3 shallots, chopped
2 kaffir lime leaves, mid-rib removed, shredded
1 tbsp oil to blend

1 To make the curry paste, grind all the ingredients together in a large pestle and mortar, food processor or grinder. The paste will keep for up to three weeks in a sealed jar in the refrigerator.

2 Put a wok or large, heavy frying pan (skillet) over a high heat, add the red curry paste and stir until fragrant. Reduce the heat.

3 Add the coconut milk, lime leaf, light soy sauce, baby corn, broccoli, beans and cashew nuts. Bring to the boil and simmer for about 10 minutes until the vegetables are cooked, but still firm.

4 Remove the lime leaf and stir in the basil leaves and coriander (cilantro). Serve over rice, garnished with peanuts.

Step *1*

Step *3*

Step *4*

Vegetable Medley

*Serve this as a crisp and colourful vegetarian dish, with pitta bread,
chapattis or naan, or as an accompaniment to roast or grilled meats.*

SERVES 4

INGREDIENTS

150 g/5 oz young, tender French (green) beans
8 baby carrots
6 baby turnips
½ small cauliflower
2 tbsp vegetable oil
2 large onions, sliced
2 garlic cloves, chopped finely
300 ml/½ pint/1¼ cups natural yogurt
1 tbsp cornflour (cornstarch)
2 tbsp tomato purée (paste)
large pinch of chilli powder
salt

1 Top and tail the beans and snap them in half. Cut the carrots in half and the turnips in quarters. Divide the cauliflower into florets, discarding the thick stalk.

2 Steam the vegetables over boiling, salted water for 3 minutes, then turn them into a colander and plunge them at once in a large bowl of cold water to prevent further cooking.

3 Heat the oil in a pan and fry the onions until they are translucent. Stir in the garlic and cook for 1 further minute.

4 Mix together the yogurt, cornflour (cornstarch) and tomato purée (paste) to form a smooth paste. Stir this paste into the onions in the pan and cook for 1-2 minutes until the sauce is well blended.

5 Drain the vegetables well, then gradually stir them into the sauce, taking care not to break them up. Season with salt and chilli powder to taste, cover and simmer gently for 5 minutes, until the vegetables are just tender. Taste and adjust the seasoning if necessary. Serve immediately.

Step *2*

Step *4*

Step *5*

Sweetcorn Patties

These are a delicious addition to any party buffet, and very simple to prepare. Serve with a sweet chilli sauce.

MAKES 12

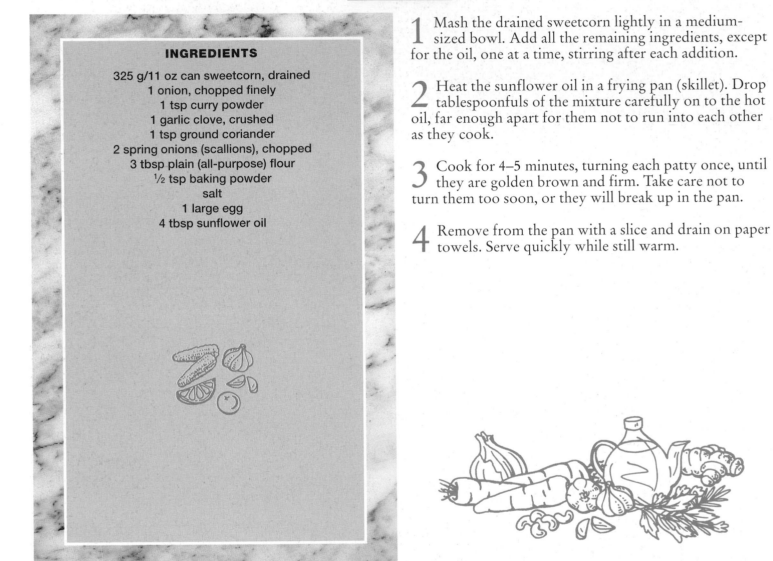

INGREDIENTS

325 g/11 oz can sweetcorn, drained
1 onion, chopped finely
1 tsp curry powder
1 garlic clove, crushed
1 tsp ground coriander
2 spring onions (scallions), chopped
3 tbsp plain (all-purpose) flour
½ tsp baking powder
salt
1 large egg
4 tbsp sunflower oil

1 Mash the drained sweetcorn lightly in a medium-sized bowl. Add all the remaining ingredients, except for the oil, one at a time, stirring after each addition.

2 Heat the sunflower oil in a frying pan (skillet). Drop tablespoonfuls of the mixture carefully on to the hot oil, far enough apart for them not to run into each other as they cook.

3 Cook for 4–5 minutes, turning each patty once, until they are golden brown and firm. Take care not to turn them too soon, or they will break up in the pan.

4 Remove from the pan with a slice and drain on paper towels. Serve quickly while still warm.

Step *1*

Step *2*

Step *3*

Three Mushrooms in Coconut Milk

*A filling and tasty main course dish
served over rice or noodles.*

SERVES 4

INGREDIENTS

2 lemon grass stalks, sliced thinly
2 green chillies, deseeded
and chopped finely
1 tbsp light soy sauce
2 garlic cloves, crushed
2 tbsp chopped fresh coriander (cilantro)
2 tbsp chopped fresh parsley
6 slices galangal, peeled
3 tbsp sunflower oil
1 aubergine (eggplant), cubed
60 g/2 oz/²⁄₃ cup oyster mushrooms
60 g/2 oz/²⁄₃ cup chestnut (crimini) mushrooms
60 g/2 oz/²⁄₃ cup field mushrooms,
quartered if large
125 g/4 oz French (green) beans,
cut into 5 cm/2 inch lengths, blanched
300 ml/¹⁄₂ pint/1¹⁄₄ cups coconut milk
1 tbsp lemon juice
rice, to serve
2 tbsp chopped roasted peanuts, to garnish

1 Grind together the lemon grass, chillies, soy sauce, garlic, coriander (cilantro), parsley and galangal in a large pestle and mortar or a food processor. Set aside.

2 Heat the sunflower oil in a wok or large, heavy frying pan (skillet). Add the aubergine (eggplant) and stir over a high heat for 3 minutes, then stir in the mushrooms and beans. Cook for 3 minutes, stirring constantly. Add the ground spice paste.

3 Add the coconut milk and lemon juice to the pan, bring to the boil and simmer for 2 minutes.

4 Serve immediately over rice, and garnish with the roasted peanuts.

Step *1*

Step *2*

Step *3*

Stir-Fried Winter Vegetables with Coriander (Cilantro)

Ordinary winter vegetables are given extraordinary treatment in this lively stir-fry, just the thing for perking up jaded palates.

SERVES 4

INGREDIENTS

3 tbsp sesame oil
30 g/1 oz/¼ cup blanched almonds
1 large carrot, cut into thin strips
1 large turnip, cut into thin strips
1 onion, sliced finely
1 garlic clove, crushed
3 celery sticks, sliced finely
125 g/4 oz Brussels sprouts, trimmed and halved
125 g/4 oz cauliflower, broken into florets
125 g/4 oz/2 cups white cabbage, shredded
2 tsp sesame seeds
1 tsp grated fresh root ginger
½ tsp medium chilli powder
1 tbsp chopped fresh coriander (cilantro)
1 tbsp light soy sauce
salt and pepper
sprigs of fresh coriander (cilantro), to garnish

1 Heat the sesame oil in a wok or large frying pan (skillet). Stir-fry the almonds until lightly browned, then lift them out and drain on paper towels.

2 Add all the vegetables to the wok or frying pan (skillet), except for the cabbage. Stir-fry briskly for 3–4 minutes.

3 Add the cabbage, sesame seeds, ginger and chilli powder to the vegetables and cook, stirring, for 2 minutes.

4 Add the chopped coriander (cilantro), soy sauce and almonds to the mixture, stirring them through gently. Serve the vegetables, garnished with sprigs of fresh coriander (cilantro).

Step *1*

Step *3*

Step *4*

Courgette (Zucchini), Carrot & Feta Cheese Patties

Grated carrots, courgettes (zucchini) and Feta cheese are combined with cumin seeds, poppy seeds, curry powder and chopped fresh parsley.

SERVES 4

INGREDIENTS:

2 large carrots
1 large courgette (zucchini)
1 small onion
60 g/2 oz Feta cheese
30 g/1 oz/¼ cup plain (all-purpose) flour
¼ tsp cumin seeds
½ tsp poppy seeds
1 tsp medium curry powder
1 tbsp chopped fresh parsley
1 egg, beaten
30 g/1 oz/2 tbsp butter
2 tbsp vegetable oil
salt and pepper
sprigs of fresh herbs, to garnish

1 Grate the carrots, courgette (zucchini), onion and Feta cheese coarsely, either by hand or in a food processor.

2 Mix together the flour, cumin seeds, poppy seeds, curry powder and parsley in a large bowl. Season well with salt and pepper.

3 Add the carrot mixture to the seasoned flour, tossing well to combine. Stir in the beaten egg and mix well.

4 Heat the butter and oil in a large frying pan (skillet). Place heaped tablespoonfuls of the carrot mixture in the pan, flattening them slightly with the back of the spoon. Fry gently for about 2 minutes on each side, until crisp and golden brown. Drain on paper towels and keep warm until all the mixture is used.

5 Serve, garnished with sprigs of fresh herbs.

Step *2*

Step *3*

Step *4*

Indonesian Chestnut & Vegetable Stir-Fry with Peanut Sauce

This colourful, spicy stir-fry has an Indonesian influence, with the shallots, chillies, ginger, fresh coriander (cilantro) and limes.

SERVES 4

INGREDIENTS

SAUCE

125 g/4 oz/1 cup unsalted roasted peanuts
2 tsp hot chilli sauce
180 ml/6 fl oz/³⁄₄ cup coconut milk
2 tbsp soy sauce
1 tbsp ground coriander
pinch of ground turmeric
1 tbsp dark muscovado sugar

STIR-FRY

3 tbsp sesame oil
3–4 shallots, finely sliced
1 garlic clove, finely sliced
1–2 red chillies, deseeded and finely chopped
1 large carrot, cut into fine strips
1 yellow and 1 red (bell) pepper, sliced
1 courgette (zucchini), cut into fine strips
125 g/4 oz sugar–snap peas, trimmed
7.5 cm/3 inch piece of cucumber,
cut into strips
250 g/8 oz oyster mushrooms,
250 g/8 oz canned chestnuts, drained
2 tsp grated ginger root
finely grated rind and juice of 1 lime
1 tbsp chopped fresh coriander (cilantro)
salt and pepper
slices of lime, to garnish

1 To make the sauce, grind the peanuts in a blender, or chop very finely. Put into a small pan with the remaining ingredients. Heat gently and simmer for 3–4 minutes.

2 Heat the sesame oil in a wok or large frying pan (skillet). Add the shallots, garlic and chillies and stir-fry for 2 minutes.

3 Add the carrot, (bell) peppers, courgette (zucchini) and sugar–snap peas to the wok or pan (skillet) and stir-fry for 2 more minutes.

4 Add all the remaining ingredients to the wok or pan (skillet) and stir-fry briskly for about 5 minutes, or until the vegetables are crisp, yet crunchy.

5 Divide the stir-fry between four warmed serving plates, and garnish with slices of lime. Serve with the peanut sauce.

 Step *1*

Step *3*

Step *4*

Green Curry with Tempeh

Green curry paste will keep for up to three weeks in the refrigerator.
Serve over rice or noodles.

SERVES 4

INGREDIENTS

1 tbsp sunflower oil
175 g/6 oz marinated or plain tempeh,
cut into diamonds
6 spring onions (scallions),
cut into 2.5 cm/1 inch pieces
150 ml/¼ pint/⅔ cup coconut milk
6 tbsp Green Curry Paste
grated rind of 1 lime
15 g/½ oz/¼ cup fresh basil leaves
¼ tsp liquid seasoning, such as Maggi

GREEN CURRY PASTE

2 tsp coriander seeds
1 tsp cumin seeds
1 tsp black peppercorns
4 large green chillies, deseeded
2 shallots, quartered
2 garlic cloves, peeled
2 tbsp chopped fresh coriander (cilantro),
including root and stalk
grated rind of 1 lime
1 tbsp roughly chopped galangal
1 tsp ground turmeric
salt
2 tbsp oil

TO GARNISH

fresh coriander (cilantro) leaves
2 green chillies, sliced thinly

1 To make the green curry paste, grind together the coriander and cumin seeds and the peppercorns in a food processor or pestle and mortar.

2 Blend the remaining ingredients together and add the ground spice mixture. Store in a clean, dry jar for up to 3 weeks in the refrigerator, or freeze in a suitable container.

3 Heat the oil in a wok or large, heavy frying pan (skillet). Add the tempeh and stir over a high heat for about 2 minutes until sealed on all sides. Add the spring onions (scallions) and stir-fry for 1 minute. Remove the tempeh and spring onions (scallions) and reserve.

4 Put half the coconut milk into the wok or pan (skillet) and bring to the boil. Add the curry paste and lime rind, and cook until fragrant, about 1 minute. Add the reserved tempeh and spring onions (scallions).

5 Add the remaining coconut milk and simmer for 7–8 minutes. Stir in the basil leaves and liquid seasoning. Simmer for one more minute before serving, garnished with coriander (cilantro) and chillies.

 Step *3*

Step *4*

Step *5*

Cauliflower with Oriental Greens

This is a delicious way to cook cauliflower –
even without the greens.

SERVES 4

INGREDIENTS

175 g/6 oz cauliflower, cut into florets
1 garlic clove
½ tsp turmeric
1 tbsp coriander (cilantro) root or stem
1 tbsp sunflower oil
2 spring onions (scallions),
cut into 2.5 cm/1 inch pieces
125 g/4 oz oriental greens, such as Thai
spinach, bok choy or mustard greens,
tough stalks removed
1 tsp yellow mustard seeds

1 Blanch the cauliflower, rinse in cold running water and drain. Set aside.

2 Grind the garlic, turmeric and coriander (cilantro) root or stem together in a pestle and mortar or spice grinder.

3 Heat the oil in a wok or large, heavy frying pan (skillet). Add the spring onions (scallions) and stir over a high heat for 2 minutes. Add the greens and stir for 1 minute. Set aside.

4 Return the wok or frying pan (skillet) to the heat and add the mustard seeds. Stir until they start to pop, then add the turmeric mixture and the cauliflower, and stir until all the cauliflower is coated. Serve with the greens on a warmed serving plate.

Step *2*

Step *3*

Step *4*

CASSEROLES, BAKES & ROASTS

Anyone who ever thought that vegetarian meals were dull will be proved wrong by the rich variety of dishes in this chapter. You'll recognize influences from Indian, Mexican and Chinese cooking, but there are also traditional stews and casseroles as well as hearty bakes and roasts. They all make exciting eating at any time of year, on virtually any occasion.

There are ideas for midweek meals or for entertaining, some traditional and some more unusual. Try Winter Vegetable Cobbler (page 198) as a sustaining but economical family supper, or Indian Curry Feast (page 188) for a special Saturday night dinner with friends. Some of the ingredients may be unfamiliar but you should have no difficulty in buying them. Don't be afraid to substitute where appropriate. For instance, you may prefer to make the Almond & Sesame Nut Roast (page 196) with peanuts instead of almonds for a more economical everyday occasion. There is no reason why you cannot enjoy experimenting and adding your own touch to these imaginative ideas.

Green Vegetable Gougère

A tasty, simple supper dish of choux pastry and crisp green vegetables.
The choux pastry ring can be filled with all kinds of vegetables.

SERVES 4

INGREDIENTS

150 g/5 oz/1¼ cups plain (all-purpose) flour
125 g/4 oz/½ cup butter or margarine
300 ml/½ pint/1¼ cups water
4 eggs, beaten
90 g/3 oz/¾ cup grated Gruyère cheese
1 tbsp milk
salt and pepper

FILLING

30 g/1 oz/2 tbsp garlic and herb butter
or margarine
2 tsp olive oil
2 leeks, shredded
250 g/8 oz green cabbage, shredded finely
125 g/4 oz/2 cups bean-sprouts
½ tsp grated lime rind
1 tbsp lime juice
celery salt and pepper
lime slices, to garnish

1 Sift the flour on to a piece of baking parchment and set aside. Cut the butter or margarine into dice and put in a saucepan with the water. Heat until the butter has melted.

2 Bring the butter and water to the boil, then shoot in the flour all at once. Beat until the mixture becomes thick. Remove from the heat and beat until the mixture is glossy and comes away from the sides of the saucepan.

3 Transfer to a mixing bowl and cool for 10 minutes. Gradually beat in the eggs, a little at a time, making sure they are thoroughly incorporated after each addition. Stir in 60 g/2 oz/½ cup of the cheese and season.

4 Dampen a baking sheet (cookie sheet). Place spoonfuls of the mixture in a 23 cm/9 inch circle on the baking sheet (cookie sheet). Brush with milk and sprinkle with the remaining cheese. Bake in a preheated oven, 220°C/425°F/Gas Mark 7, for 30–35 minutes until golden and crisp. Transfer to a warmed serving plate.

5 Make the filling about 5 minutes before the end of cooking time. Heat the butter or margarine and the oil in a large frying pan (skillet) and stir-fry the leeks and cabbage for 2 minutes.

6 Add the bean-sprouts, lime rind and juice and cook for 1 minute, stirring. Season to taste, then pile into the centre of the cooked pastry ring. Garnish with lime slices and serve.

Step *2*

Step *3*

Step *4*

Lentil Roast

The perfect dish to serve for an alternative Sunday lunch.
Roast vegetables make a succulent accompaniment.

SERVES 6

INGREDIENTS

250 g/8 oz/1 cup red lentils
500 ml/16 fl oz/2 cups Fresh Vegetable
Stock (page 12)
1 bay leaf
15 g/½ oz/1 tbsp butter or margarine,
softened
2 tbsp dried wholemeal (whole wheat)
breadcrumbs
250 g/8 oz/2 cups grated mature
(sharp) Cheddar
1 leek, chopped finely
125 g/4 oz button mushrooms,
chopped finely
90 g/3 oz/1½ cups fresh wholemeal
(whole wheat) breadcrumbs
2 tbsp chopped fresh parsley
1 tbsp lemon juice
2 eggs, beaten lightly
salt and pepper
sprigs of fresh flat-leaf parsley, to garnish
mixed roast vegetables, to serve

1 Put the lentils, stock and bay leaf in a saucepan. Bring to the boil, cover and simmer gently for 15–20 minutes until all the liquid is absorbed and the lentils have softened. Discard the bay leaf.

2 Meanwhile, base-line a 1 kg/2 lb loaf tin (pan) with baking parchment. Grease with the butter or margarine and sprinkle with the dried breadcrumbs.

3 Stir the cheese, leek, mushrooms, fresh breadcrumbs and parsley into the lentils.

4 Bind the mixture together with the lemon juice and eggs. Season well and spoon into the prepared loaf tin (pan). Smooth the top and bake in a preheated oven, 190°C/375°F/Gas Mark 5, for 1 hour until golden.

5 Loosen the loaf with a palette knife (spatula) and turn on to a warmed serving plate. Garnish with parsley and serve sliced, with roast vegetables.

Step *2*

Step *3*

Step *4*

Red Bean Stew & Dumplings

There's nothing better on a cold day than a hearty dish topped with dumplings. This recipe is quick and easy to prepare.

SERVES 4

INGREDIENTS

1 tbsp vegetable oil
1 red onion, sliced
2 celery stalks, chopped
900 ml/1½ pints/3½ cups Fresh Vegetable
Stock (page 12)
250 g/8 oz carrots, diced
250 g/8 oz potatoes, diced
250 g/8 oz courgettes (zucchini), diced
4 tomatoes, peeled and chopped
125 g/4 oz/½ cup red lentils
425 g/14 oz can kidney beans,
rinsed and drained
1 tsp paprika
salt and pepper

DUMPLINGS

125 g/4 oz/1 cup plain (all-purpose) flour
½ tsp salt
2 tsp baking powder
1 tsp paprika
1 tsp dried mixed herbs
30 g/1 oz/2 tbsp vegetable suet
7 tbsp water
sprigs of fresh flat-leaf parsley, to garnish

1 Heat the oil in a flameproof casserole or a large saucepan and gently fry the onion and celery for 3–4 minutes until just softened.

2 Pour in the stock and stir in the carrots and potatoes. Bring to the boil, cover and cook for 5 minutes.

3 Stir in the courgettes (zucchini), tomatoes, lentils, kidney beans, paprika and seasoning. Bring to the boil, cover and cook for 5 minutes.

4 Meanwhile, make the dumplings. Sift the flour, salt, baking powder and paprika into a bowl. Stir in the herbs and suet. Bind together with the water to form a soft dough. Divide into eight and roll into balls.

5 Uncover the stew, stir, then add the dumplings, pushing them slightly into the stew. Cover and reduce the heat to a simmer. Cook for a further 15 minutes until the dumplings have risen and are cooked through. Garnish with flat-leaf parsley and serve immediately.

Step 2

Step 4

Step 5

Mushroom & Nut Crumble

A filling, tasty dish that is ideal for a warming family supper.
The crunchy topping is flavoured with three different types of nuts.

SERVES 4

INGREDIENTS

350 g/12 oz open-cup mushrooms, sliced
350 g/12 oz chestnut mushrooms, sliced
400 ml/14 fl oz/1¾ cups Fresh Vegetable
Stock (page 12)
60 g/2 oz/¼ cup butter or margarine
1 large onion, chopped finely
1 garlic clove, crushed
60 g/2 oz/½ cup plain (all-purpose) flour
4 tbsp double (heavy) cream
2 tbsp chopped fresh parsley
salt and pepper
fresh herbs, to garnish

CRUMBLE TOPPING

90 g/3 oz/¾ cup medium oatmeal
90 g/3 oz/¾ cup wholemeal (whole wheat) flour
30 g/1 oz/¼ cup ground almonds
30 g/1 oz/¼ cup finely chopped walnuts
60 g/2 oz/½ cup finely chopped unsalted shelled
pistachio nuts
1 tsp dried thyme
90 g/3 oz/⅓ cup butter or margarine, softened
1 tbsp fennel seeds

1 Put the mushrooms and stock in a large saucepan, bring to the boil, cover and simmer for 15 minutes until tender. Drain, reserving the stock.

2 In another saucepan, melt the butter or margarine, and gently fry the onion and garlic for 2–3 minutes until just softened but not browned. Stir in the flour and cook for 1 minute.

3 Remove from the heat and gradually stir in the reserved mushroom stock. Return to the heat and cook, stirring, until thickened. Stir in the mushrooms, seasoning, cream and parsley and spoon into a shallow ovenproof dish.

4 To make the topping, mix together the oatmeal, flour, nuts, thyme and plenty of seasoning.

5 Using a fork, mix in the butter or margarine until the topping resembles coarse breadcrumbs.

6 Sprinkle the mixture over the mushrooms, sprinkle with fennel seeds and bake in a preheated oven, 190°C/375°F/Gas Mark 5, for 25–30 minutes until golden and crisp. Garnish with herbs and serve.

 1

 3

Step *6*

Indian Curry Feast

This vegetable curry is quick and easy to prepare, and it tastes superb.
A colourful Indian salad and a mint raita make perfect accompaniments.

SERVES 4

INGREDIENTS

1 tbsp vegetable oil
2 garlic cloves, crushed
1 onion, chopped
3 celery stalks, sliced
1 apple, chopped
1 tbsp medium-strength curry powder
1 tsp ground ginger
425 g/14 oz can chick-peas (garbanzo beans)
125 g/4 oz dwarf green beans, sliced
250 g/8 oz cauliflower, broken into florets
250 g/8 oz potatoes, cut into cubes
175 g/6 oz/2 cups mushrooms, wiped and sliced
600 ml/1 pint/2½ cups Fresh Vegetable
Stock (page 12)
1 tbsp tomato purée (paste)
30 g/1 oz sultanas (golden raisins)
175 g/6 oz/scant 1 cup basmati rice
1 tbsp garam masala

SALAD

4 tomatoes, chopped
1 green chilli, deseeded and finely chopped
7 cm/3 inch piece of cucumber, chopped
1 tbsp fresh coriander (cilantro)
4 spring onions (scallions), trimmed and chopped

MINT RAITA

150 ml/¼ pint/⅔ cup natural yogurt
1 tbsp chopped fresh mint

1 Heat the oil in a large saucepan and fry the garlic, onion, celery and apple gently for 3–4 minutes. Add the curry powder and ginger, and cook gently for 1 more minute.

2 Drain the chick-peas (gabanzo beans) and add to the onion mixture with the remaining ingredients except the rice and garam masala. Bring to the boil, then reduce the heat. Cover and simmer for 35–40 minutes.

3 To make the salad, combine all the ingredients. Cover and chill.

4 To make the raita, mix the yogurt and mint together. Transfer to a serving dish, then cover and chill.

5 Cook the rice in boiling, lightly salted water until just tender, according to the instructions on the packet. Drain thoroughly.

6 Just before serving, stir the garam masala into the curry. Divide between four warmed serving plates, and serve with the salad, mint raita and rice. Garnish the raita with fresh mint.

 1

 2

Step *4*

Root Croustades with Sunshine Peppers

This colourful combination of grated root vegetables and mixed (bell) peppers would make a stunning dinner-party dish.

SERVES 4

INGREDIENTS

1 orange (bell) pepper
1 red (bell) pepper
1 yellow (bell) pepper
3 tbsp olive oil
2 tbsp red wine vinegar
1 tsp French mustard
1 tsp clear honey
salt and pepper
sprigs of fresh flat-leaf parsley, to garnish
green vegetables, to serve

CROUSTADES

250 g/8 oz potatoes, grated coarsely
250 g/8 oz carrots, grated coarsely
350 g/12 oz celeriac (celery root), grated coarsely
1 garlic clove, crushed
1 tbsp lemon juice
30 g/1 oz/2 tbsp butter or margarine, melted
1 egg, beaten
1 tbsp vegetable oil

1 Place the (bell) peppers on a baking sheet and bake in a preheated oven, 190°C/375°F/Gas Mark 5, for 35 minutes, turning after 20 minutes.

2 Cover with a tea towel (dish cloth) and leave to cool for 10 minutes.

3 Peel the skin from the cooked (bell) peppers; cut in half and discard the seeds. Thinly slice the flesh into strips and place in a shallow dish.

4 Put the oil, vinegar, mustard, honey and seasoning in a small screw-top jar and shake well to mix. Pour over the (bell) pepper strips, mix well and leave to marinate for 2 hours.

5 To make the croustades, put the potatoes, carrots and celeriac (celery root) in a mixing bowl and toss in the garlic and lemon juice.

6 Mix in the melted butter or margarine and the egg. Season well. Divide the mixture into eight and pile on to two baking sheets (cookie sheets) lined with baking parchment, forming each into a 10 cm/ 4 inch round. Brush with oil.

7 Bake in a preheated oven, 220°C/ 425°F/Gas Mark 7, for 30–35 minutes until crisp around the edge and golden. Carefully transfer to a warmed serving dish. Heat the (bell) peppers and the marinade for 2–3 minutes until warmed through. Spoon the (bell) peppers over the croustades, garnish with parsley and serve with green vegetables.

Step *3*

Step *5*

Step *6*

Spicy Stuffed Chinese Leaves

*Mushrooms, spring onions (scallions), celery and rice are flavoured with
five-spice powder and wrapped in Chinese leaves.*

SERVES 4

INGREDIENTS

8 large Chinese leaves
60 g/2 oz/⅓ cup long-grain rice
½ vegetable stock (bouillon) cube
60 g/2 oz/¼ cup butter
1 bunch spring onions (scallions),
trimmed and chopped finely
1 celery stalk, chopped finely
125 g/4 oz/1¼ cups button mushrooms, sliced
1 tsp Chinese five-spice powder
300 ml/½ pint/1¼ cups passatta
(sieved tomato sauce)
salt and pepper
fresh chives, to garnish

1 Blanch the Chinese leaves in boiling water for 1
minute. Refresh them under cold running water and
drain well. Be careful not to tear them.

2 Cook the rice in plenty of boiling water, with the
stock (bouillon) cube, until just tender. Drain well.

3 Meanwhile, melt the butter in a frying pan (skillet)
and fry the spring onions (scallions) and celery gently
for 3–4 minutes until softened, but not browned. Add the
mushrooms and cook for a further 3–4 minutes, stirring
frequently.

4 Add the cooked rice to the pan with the five-spice
powder. Season with salt and pepper and stir well to
combine the ingredients.

5 Lay out the Chinese leaves on a work surface
(counter) and divide the rice mixture between them.
Roll each leaf into a neat parcel to enclose the stuffing.
Place them, seam-side down, in a greased ovenproof dish.
Pour the passatta over them and cover with foil.

6 Bake in a preheated oven, 190°C/375°F/Gas Mark 5,
for 25–30 minutes. Serve immediately, garnished with
fresh chives.

Step *1*

Step *4*

Step *5*

Savoury Bread & Butter Pudding

Quick, simple and nutritious –
what more could you ask for an inexpensive mid-week meal?

SERVES 4

INGREDIENTS

60 g/2 oz/¼ cup butter or margarine
1 bunch spring onions (scallions),
sliced
6 slices of white or brown bread,
crusts removed
175g/6 oz/1½ cups grated mature (sharp) Cheddar
2 eggs
450 ml/¾ pint/scant 2 cups milk
salt and pepper
sprigs of fresh flat-leaf parsley, to garnish

1 Grease a 1.5 litre/2½ pint/1½ quart baking dish with a little of the butter or margarine. Melt the remaining butter or margarine in a small saucepan and fry the spring onions (scallions) until softened and golden.

2 Meanwhile, cut the bread into triangles and layer half of them in the baking dish. Top with the spring onions (scallions) and half the cheese.

3 Beat together the eggs and milk and season with salt and pepper. Layer the remaining triangles of bread in the dish and carefully pour over the milk mixture. Leave to soak for 15–20 minutes.

4 Sprinkle the remaining cheese over the soaked bread. Bake in a preheated oven, 190°C/375°F/Gas Mark 5, for 35–40 minutes until puffed up and golden brown. Garnish with flat-leaf parsley and serve at once.

Step *2*

Step *3*

Step *4*

Almond & Sesame Nut Roast

Toasted almonds are combined with sesame seeds, rice and vegetables in this tasty vegetarian roast. Serve it with a delicious onion and mushroom sauce.

SERVES 4

INGREDIENTS

2 tbsp sesame or olive oil
1 small onion, chopped finely
60 g/2 oz/scant ¼ cup risotto rice
300 ml/½ pint/1¼ cups Fresh Vegetable
Stock (page 12)
1 large carrot, grated
1 large leek, trimmed and chopped finely
2 tsp sesame seeds, toasted
90 g/3 oz/¾ cup chopped almonds, toasted
60 g/2 oz/½ cup ground almonds
90 g/3 oz/¾ cup mature (sharp)
Cheddar, grated
2 eggs, beaten
1 tsp dried mixed herbs
salt and pepper
sprigs of flat-leaf parsley, to garnish
fresh vegetables, to serve

SAUCE

30 g/1 oz/2 tbsp butter
1 small onion, chopped finely
125 g/4 oz/1¼ cup mushrooms, chopped finely
30 g/1 oz/¼ cup plain (all-purpose) flour
300 ml/½ pint/1½ cups Fresh Vegetable
Stock (page 12)

1 Heat the oil in a large frying pan (skillet) and fry the onion gently for 2–3 minutes. Add the rice and cook gently for 5–6 minutes, stirring frequently.

2 Add the vegetable stock, bring to the boil and then simmer for about 15 minutes, or until the rice is tender. Add a little extra water if necessary. Remove from the heat and transfer to a large mixing bowl.

3 Add the carrot, leek, sesame seeds, almonds, cheese, beaten eggs and herbs to the mixture. Mix well and season with salt and pepper. Transfer the mixture to a greased 500 g/1 lb loaf tin, levelling the surface. Bake in a preheated oven, 180°C/350°F/Gas Mark 4, for about 1 hour, until set and firm. Leave in the tin for 10 minutes.

4 To make the sauce, melt the butter in a small saucepan and fry the onion until dark golden brown. Add the mushrooms and cook for a further 2 minutes. Stir in the flour, cook gently for 1 minute and then gradually add the stock. Bring to the boil, stirring constantly, until thickened and blended. Season to taste.

5 Turn out the nut roast, slice and serve on warmed plates with fresh vegetables, accompanied by the sauce. Garnish with sprigs of flat-leaf parsley.

Step *1*

Step *3*

Step *4*

Winter Vegetable Cobbler

Seasonal fresh vegetables are casseroled with lentils then topped with a ring of fresh cheese scones (biscuits) to make this tasty cobbler.

SERVES 4

INGREDIENTS

1 tbsp olive oil
1 garlic clove, crushed
8 small onions, halved
2 celery stalks, sliced
250 g/8 oz swede (rutabaga), chopped
2 carrots, sliced
½ small cauliflower, broken into florets
250 g/8 oz mushrooms, sliced
425 g/14 oz can chopped tomatoes
60 g/2 oz/¼ cup red lentils
2 tbsp cornflour (cornstarch)
3–4 tbsp water
300 ml/½ pint/1¼ cups Fresh Vegetable
Stock (page 12)
2 tsp Tabasco sauce
2 tsp chopped fresh oregano or parsley
sprigs of oregano, to garnish

COBBLER TOPPING

250 g/8 oz/2 cups self-raising flour
60 g/2 oz/¼ cup butter
125 g/4 oz/1 cup grated mature
(sharp) Cheddar
2 tsp chopped fresh oregano or parsley
1 egg, beaten
150 ml/¼ pint/⅔ cup skimmed milk
salt

1 Heat the oil in a large saucepan and fry the garlic and onions for 5 minutes. Add the celery, swede (rutabaga), carrots and cauliflower and fry for 2–3 minutes more.

2 Remove from the heat and add the mushrooms, tomatoes and lentils. Mix the cornflour (cornstarch) with the water and add to the pan with the vegetable stock, Tabasco sauce and oregano or parsley. Bring to the boil, stirring, until thickened. Transfer to an ovenproof dish, cover and bake in a preheated oven, 180°C/350°F/Gas Mark 4, for 20 minutes.

3 To make the topping, sift the flour and salt into a bowl. Rub in the butter, then stir in most of the cheese and the chopped herbs. Beat together the egg and milk and add enough to the dry ingredients to make a soft dough. Knead lightly, roll out to 1 cm/½inch thick and cut into 5 cm/2 inch rounds.

4 Remove the dish from the oven and increase the temperature to 200°C/400°F/Gas Mark 6. Arrange the rounds around the edge of the dish, brush with the remaining egg and milk and sprinkle with the reserved cheese. Cook for a further 10–12 minutes until the topping is risen and golden. Garnish and serve at once.

Step *2*

Step *3*

Step *4*

Creamy Baked Fennel

Fennel tastes fabulous in this creamy sauce, flavoured with caraway seeds.
A crunchy breadcrumb topping gives an interesting change of texture.

SERVES 4

INGREDIENTS

2 tbsp lemon juice
2 bulbs fennel, trimmed
125 g/4 oz/¼ cup low-fat soft cheese
150 ml/¼ pint/⅔ cup single (light)
cream
150 ml/¼ pint/⅔ cup milk
1 egg, beaten
60 g/2 oz/¼ cup butter
2 tsp caraway seeds
60 g/2 oz/1 cup fresh white breadcrumbs
salt and pepper
sprigs of parsley, to garnish

1 Bring a large saucepan of water to the boil and add the lemon juice. Slice the bulbs of fennel thinly and add them to the saucepan. Cook for 2–3 minutes to blanch, and then drain them well, and arrange in a buttered ovenproof baking dish.

2 Beat the soft cheese in a bowl until smooth. Add the cream, milk and beaten egg, and whisk together until combined. Season with salt and pepper and pour the mixture over the fennel.

3 Melt 15 g/½ oz of the butter in a small frying pan (skillet) and fry the caraway seeds gently for 1–2 minutes, to release their flavour and aroma. Sprinkle them over the fennel.

4 Melt the remaining butter in a frying pan (skillet). Add the breadcrumbs and fry gently until lightly browned. Sprinkle evenly over the surface of the fennel.

5 Place in a preheated oven, 180°C/350°F/Gas Mark 4, and bake for 25–30 minutes, or until the fennel is tender. Serve, garnished with sprigs of parsley.

 Step *1*

 Step *2*

Step *4*

Spinach Pancake Layer

Nutty-tasting buckwheat pancakes are combined with a cheesy spinach
mixture and baked with a crispy topping.

SERVES 4

INGREDIENTS

125 g/4 oz/1 cup buckwheat flour
1 egg, beaten
1 tbsp walnut oil
300 ml/½ pint/1¼ cups milk
2 tsp vegetable oil

FILLING

1 kg/2 lb young spinach leaves
2 tbsp water
1 bunch spring onions (scallions),
white and green parts, chopped
2 tsp walnut oil
1 egg, beaten
1 egg yolk
250 g/8 oz/1 cup cottage cheese
½ tsp grated nutmeg
30 g/1 oz/¼ cup grated mature (sharp) Cheddar
30 g/1 oz/¼ cup walnut pieces
salt and pepper

1 Sift the flour into a bowl and add any husks that remain behind in the sieve (strainer).

2 Make a well in the centre and add the egg and walnut oil. Gradually whisk in the milk to make a smooth batter. Leave to stand for 30 minutes.

3 To make the filling, wash the spinach and pack into a saucepan with the water. Cover tightly and cook on a high heat for 5–6 minutes until soft.

4 Drain well and leave to cool. Gently fry the spring onions (scallions) in the walnut oil for 2–3 minutes until just soft. Drain on paper towels. Set aside.

5 Whisk the batter. Brush a small crêpe pan with oil, heat until hot and pour in enough batter to lightly cover the base. Cook for 1–2 minutes until set, turn and cook for 1 minute until golden. Turn on to a warmed plate. Repeat to make 8–10 pancakes, layering them with baking parchment.

6 Chop the spinach and dry with paper towels. Mix with the spring onions (scallions), beaten egg, egg yolk, cottage cheese, nutmeg and seasoning.

7 Layer the pancakes and spinach mixture on a baking sheet lined with baking parchment, finishing with a pancake. Sprinkle with Cheddar cheese and bake in a preheated oven, 190°C/375°F/Gas Mark 5, for 20–25 minutes until firm and golden. Sprinkle with the walnuts and serve.

Step *5*

Step *6*

Step *7*

Coconut Vegetable Curry

A mildly spiced but richly flavoured Indian-style dish full of different textures and flavours. Serve with naan bread to soak up the tasty sauce.

SERVES 6

INGREDIENTS

1 large aubergine (eggplant),
cut into 2.5 cm/1 inch cubes
2 tbsp salt
2 tbsp vegetable oil
2 garlic cloves, crushed
1 fresh green chilli,
deseeded and chopped finely
1 tsp grated ginger root
1 onion, chopped finely
2 tsp garam masala
8 cardamom pods
1 tsp ground turmeric
1 tbsp tomato purée (paste)
700 ml/1¼ pints/3 cups Fresh Vegetable
Stock (page 12)
1 tbsp lemon juice
250 g/8 oz potatoes, diced
250 g/8 oz small cauliflower florets
250 g/8 oz okra, trimmed
250 g/8 oz frozen peas
150 ml/¼ pint/⅔ cups coconut milk
salt and pepper
flaked coconut, to garnish
naan bread, to serve

1 Layer the aubergine (eggplant) in a bowl, sprinkling with salt as you go. Set aside for 30 minutes.

2 Rinse well under running water to remove all the salt. Drain and pat dry with paper towels. Set aside.

3 Heat the oil in a large saucepan and gently fry the garlic, chilli, ginger, onion and spices for 4–5 minutes until lightly browned.

4 Stir in the tomato purée (paste), stock, lemon juice, potatoes and cauliflower, and mix well. Bring to the boil, cover and simmer for 15 minutes.

5 Stir in the aubergine (eggplant), okra, peas and coconut milk. Adjust the seasoning. Return to the boil and continue to simmer, uncovered, for a further 10 minutes until tender. Discard the cardamom pods.

6 Pile on to a warmed serving platter, garnish with flaked coconut and serve with naan bread.

Step *1*

Step *4*

Step *5*

Mexican Chilli Corn Pie

*This bake of sweetcorn and kidney beans, flavoured with chilli and fresh
coriander (cilantro), is topped with crispy cheese cornbread.*

SERVES 4

INGREDIENTS

1 tbsp corn oil
2 garlic cloves, crushed
1 red (bell) pepper, deseeded and diced
1 green (bell) pepper, deseeded and diced
1 celery stalk, diced
1 tsp hot chilli powder
425 g/14 oz can chopped tomatoes
325 g/11 oz can sweetcorn, drained
215 g/7½ oz can kidney beans,
drained and rinsed
2 tbsp chopped fresh coriander (cilantro)
salt and pepper
sprigs of fresh coriander (cilantro), to garnish
tomato and avocado salad, to serve

TOPPING

125 g/4 oz/⅔ cup cornmeal
1 tbsp plain (all-purpose) flour
½ tsp salt
2 tsp baking powder
1 egg, beaten
90 ml/3½ fl oz/6 tbsp milk
1 tbsp corn oil
125 g/4 oz/1 cup grated mature (sharp) Cheddar

1 Heat the oil in a large frying pan (skillet) and gently fry the garlic, (bell) peppers and celery for 5–6 minutes until just softened.

2 Stir in the chilli powder, tomatoes, sweetcorn, beans and seasoning. Bring to the boil and simmer for 10 minutes. Stir in the coriander (cilantro) and spoon into an ovenproof dish.

3 To make the topping, mix together the cornmeal, flour, salt and baking powder. Make a well in the centre, add the egg, milk and oil and beat until a smooth batter is formed.

4 Spoon over the (bell) pepper and sweetcorn mixture and sprinkle with the cheese. Bake in a preheated oven, 220°C/425°F/Gas Mark 7, for 25–30 minutes until golden and firm.

5 Garnish with coriander (cilantro) sprigs and serve immediately with a tomato and avocado salad.

Step *2*

Step *3*

Step *4*

BARBECUES

If you thought vegetarian barbecues consisted of mushroom kebabs, then these recipes will convince you to think again. How about Chargrilled Vegetables with Sidekick Dressing (page 218) or Mozzarella with Barbecued Radicchio (page 232). Throughout this chapter you will find imaginative recipes that will really spice up your barbecue.

The recipes provide their fair share of protein - either from cheese, beans or tofu (bean curd). And because they all contain vegetables, they supply important vitamins, minerals and carbohydrates too.

Unless you're having a sit-down meal, easy-to-eat food is essential for barbecues. Try to choose bite-sized items that can be eaten with a fork, or stuffed self-contained items that can be eaten with the fingers. Don't forget to provide plenty of napkins.

Some preparation is needed before the barbecue starts. For instance, some foods need marinating, or threading on to skewers, but with a little forward planning you'll find plenty of time to relax with your guests.

Vine (Grape) Leaf Parcels with Soft Cheese & Almonds

A wonderful combination of soft cheese, chopped dates, ground almonds and lightly fried nuts is encased in vine (grape) leaves.

SERVES 4

INGREDIENTS

300 g/10 oz/1¼ cups full-fat soft cheese
60 g/2 oz/¼ cup ground almonds
30 g/1 oz/2 tbsp dates, pitted and chopped
30 g/1 oz/2 tbsp butter
30 g/1 oz/¼ cup flaked (slivered) almonds
12–16 vine (grape) leaves
salt and pepper
barbecued baby corn, to serve

TO GARNISH

sprigs of rosemary
tomato wedges

1 Beat the soft cheese in a large bowl. Add the ground almonds and chopped dates, and mix together thoroughly. Season with salt and pepper.

2 Melt the butter in a small frying pan (skillet). Add the flaked (slivered) almonds and fry them gently for 2–3 minutes until golden brown. Remove from the heat and leave to cool for a few minutes.

3 Mix the fried nuts with the soft cheese mixture, stirring well to combine thoroughly.

4 Soak the vine (grape) leaves in water to remove some of the saltiness, if specified on the packet. Drain them, lay them out on a work surface (counter) and spoon an equal amount of the soft cheese mixture on to each one. Fold over the leaves to enclose the filling.

5 Wrap the vine (grape) leaf parcels in foil, 1 or 2 per foil package. Place over the barbecue to heat through for about 8–10 minutes, turning once.

6 Serve with barbecued baby corn and garnish with sprigs of rosemary and tomato wedges.

Step *1*

Step *3*

Step *4*

Roasted Vegetables on Rosemary Skewers

Rosemary branches can be used as brushes for basting and as skewers.
If you buy them in a pack, look for the longest sprigs.

SERVES 6

INGREDIENTS

1 small red cabbage
1 head fennel
1 orange (bell) pepper,
cut into 3.5 cm/1½ inch dice
1 aubergine (eggplant),
halved and sliced into 1 cm/½ inch pieces
2 courgettes (zucchini),
sliced thickly diagonally
olive oil for brushing
6 rosemary twigs, about 15 cm/6 inches long,
soaked in water for 8 hours
salt and pepper

1 Put the red cabbage on its side on a chopping board and cut through the middle of the stem and heart. Divide each piece into four, including a bit of the stem in the slice to hold it together. Prepare the fennel in the same way.

2 Blanch the red cabbage and fennel in boiling water for 3 minutes, then drain well.

3 With a wooden skewer, pierce a hole through the middle of each piece of vegetable.

4 On to each rosemary twig, thread a piece of orange (bell) pepper, fennel, red cabbage, aubergine (eggplant) and courgette (zucchini), pushing the rosemary through the holes.

5 Brush liberally with olive oil and season with plenty of salt and pepper.

6 Cook over a hot barbecue for 8–10 minutes, turning occasionally. Serve hot.

Step *1*

Step *3*

Step *4*

Grilled Haloumi with Tomato & Red Onion Salad

Haloumi is a type of Cypriot cheese which remains firm and takes on a marvellous flavour when swiftly barbecued.

SERVES 4

INGREDIENTS

500 g/1 lb Haloumi, thickly sliced

ORANGE MARINADE

½ orange
60 ml/ 2 fl oz/¼ cup olive oil
2 tbsp dry white wine
2 tbsp white wine vinegar
½ tbsp snipped fresh chives
½ tbsp chopped fresh marjoram
salt and pepper

SALAD

250 g/8 oz plum tomatoes
1 small red onion
4 tbsp olive oil
2 tbsp cider vinegar
1 tsp lemon juice
pinch of ground coriander
2 tsp chopped fresh coriander (cilantro)
salt and pepper
fresh basil leaves, to garnish

1 To make the marinade, remove the rind from the orange with a zester, or grate it finely, then squeeze the juice. Mix the orange rind and juice with all the remaining ingredients in a small bowl, whisking together to combine.

2 Place the Haloumi in a shallow dish and pour the marinade over. Cover and chill for at least 30 minutes.

3 To make the salad, slice the tomatoes and arrange them on a serving plate. Slice the onion thinly and scatter over the tomatoes.

4 Whisk together the olive oil, vinegar, lemon juice, ground coriander and fresh coriander (cilantro). Season to taste with salt and pepper, then drizzle the dressing over the tomatoes and onions. Cover and chill.

5 Drain the marinade from the Haloumi. Cook the Haloumi over hot coals for 2 minutes, turning once. Transfer to plates and serve with the salad.

 Step *2*

 Step *3*

Step *4*

Barbecue Bean Burgers

*These tasty patties are ideal for a barbecue in the summer but they are
equally delicious cooked indoors at any time of year.*

SERVES 6

INGREDIENTS

125 g/4 oz/⅓ cup aduki beans
125 g/4 oz/⅓ cup black-eye beans (peas)
6 tbsp vegetable oil
1 large onion, chopped finely
1 tsp yeast extract
125 g/4 oz grated carrot
90 g/3 oz/1½ cups fresh wholemeal (whole wheat)
breadcrumbs
2 tbsp wholemeal (whole wheat) flour
salt and pepper

BARBECUE SAUCE

½ tsp chilli powder
1 tsp celery salt
2 tbsp light muscovado sugar
2 tbsp red wine vinegar
2 tbsp vegetarian Worcestershire sauce
3 tbsp tomato purée (paste)
dash of Tabasco sauce

TO SERVE

6 wholemeal (whole wheat) baps, toasted
mixed green salad
jacket potato fries

1 Place the beans in separate saucepans, cover with water and bring to the boil. Cover and simmer the aduki beans for 40 minutes and the black-eye beans (peas) for 50 minutes, until tender. Drain and rinse well.

2 Transfer to a mixing bowl and lightly mash together with a potato masher or fork. Set aside.

3 Heat 1 tablespoon of the oil in a frying pan (skillet) and gently fry the onion for 3–4 minutes until softened. Mix into the beans with the yeast extract, grated carrot, breadcrumbs and seasoning. Bind together well.

4 With wet hands, divide the mixture into 6 and form into burgers 8 cm/3½ inches in diameter. Put the flour on a plate and use to coat the burgers.

5 Heat the remaining oil in a large frying pan (skillet) and cook the burgers for 3–4 minutes on each side, turning carefully, until golden and crisp. Drain on paper towels.

6 Meanwhile, make the sauce. Mix all the ingredients together until well blended. Put the burgers in the toasted baps and serve with a mixed green salad, jacket potato fries and a spoonful of the barbecue sauce.

 Step *2*

 Step *3*

Step *4*

Chargrilled Vegetables with Sidekick Dressing

Colourful vegetables are barbecued over hot coals to make this unusual hot salad, which is served with a spicy chilli sauce on the side.

SERVES 4

INGREDIENTS

1 red (bell) pepper, cored and deseeded
1 orange or yellow (bell) pepper,
cored and deseeded
2 courgettes (zucchini)
2 corn-on-the-cob
1 aubergine (eggplant)
olive oil for brushing
chopped fresh thyme, rosemary and parsley
salt and pepper
lime or lemon wedges, to serve

DRESSING

2 tbsp olive oil
1 tbsp sesame oil
1 garlic clove, crushed
1 small onion, chopped finely
1 celery stalk, chopped finely
1 small green chilli,
deseeded and chopped finely
4 tomatoes, chopped
5 cm/2 inch piece cucumber, chopped finely
1 tbsp tomato purée (paste)
1 tbsp lime or lemon juice

1 To make the dressing, heat the olive and sesame oils together in a saucepan or frying pan (skillet). Add the garlic and onion, and fry together gently until softened, about 3 minutes.

2 Add the celery, chilli and tomatoes to the pan and cook, stirring occasionally, for 5 minutes over a medium heat.

3 Stir in the cucumber, tomato purée (paste) and lime or lemon juice, and simmer for 8–10 minutes until thick and pulpy. Season to taste with salt and pepper.

4 Cut the vegetables into thick slices and brush with a little olive oil.

5 Cook the vegetables over the hot coals for about 5–8 minutes, sprinkling them with salt and pepper and fresh herbs as they cook, and turning once.

6 Divide the vegetables between 4 serving plates and spoon some of the dressing on to the side. Serve at once, sprinkled with a few more chopped herbs and accompanied by the lime or lemon wedges.

Step *1*

Step *2*

Step *4*

Corn-on-the-Cob

*Corn-on-the-cob is available nearly all the year round,
and it can be barbecued with the husk on or off.*

SERVES 4–6

INGREDIENTS

4–6 corn-on-the-cobs
oil for brushing

TO SERVE:

butter (optional)
salt (optional)

1 Soak the cobs in hand-hot water for 20 minutes. Drain them thoroughly.

2 If the cobs have no husks, brush with oil and cook over a hot barbecue for 30 minutes, brushing occasionally with the oil and turning often.

3 If your cobs have husks, tear off all but the last two layers and brush with oil.

4 Cook over a hot barbecue for 40 minutes, brushing with oil once or twice and turning occasionally.

5 Serve hot, without the husks. If you like, add a knob of butter and salt to taste.

Step *2*

Step *3*

Step *4*

Naan Bread with Curried Vegetable Kebabs

Warmed Indian bread is served with barbecued vegetable kebabs, which are brushed with a curry-spiced yogurt baste.

SERVES 4

INGREDIENTS

naan bread, to serve
sprigs of fresh mint, to garnish

YOGURT BASTE

150 ml/¼ pint/⅔ cup natural yogurt
1 tbsp chopped fresh mint or 1 tsp dried mint
1 tsp ground cumin
1 tsp ground coriander
½ tsp chilli powder
pinch of turmeric
pinch of ground ginger
salt and pepper

KEBABS

8 small new potatoes
1 small aubergine (eggplant)
1 courgette (zucchini), cut into chunks
8 chestnut (crimini) or closed-cup mushrooms
8 small tomatoes

1 To make the spiced yogurt baste, mix together the yogurt, mint, cumin, coriander, chilli powder, turmeric and ginger. Season with salt and pepper. Cover and chill.

2 Boil the potatoes until just tender. Meanwhile, chop the aubergine (eggplant) into chunks and sprinkle them liberally with salt. Leave for 10–15 minutes to extract the bitter juices. Rinse and drain them well. Drain the potatoes.

3 Thread the vegetables on to 4 metal or wooden skewers, alternating the different types. If using wooden skewers, soak them in warm water for 30 minutes.

4 Place the skewers in a shallow dish and brush with the yogurt baste, coating them evenly. Cover and chill until ready to cook.

5 Wrap the naan bread in foil and place towards one side of the barbecue to warm through.

6 Cook the kebabs over the barbecue, basting with any remaining spiced yogurt, until they just begin to char slightly. Serve with the warmed naan bread, garnished with sprigs of fresh mint.

Step *2*

Step *3*

Step *4*

Filled Jacket Potatoes

*Cook these potatoes conventionally, wrap them in foil and keep warm at
the edge of the barbecue, ready to fill with inspired mixtures.*

SERVES 4

INGREDIENTS

4 large or 8 medium baking potatoes
paprika or chilli powder, or chopped fresh herbs,
to garnish

MEXICAN SWEETCORN RELISH

250 g/8 oz can sweetcorn, drained
½ red (bell) pepper, cored, deseeded and chopped
finely
5 cm/2 inch piece cucumber, chopped finely
½ tsp chilli powder
salt and pepper

BLUE CHEESE, CELERY & CHIVE FILLING

125 g/4 oz/½ cup full-fat soft cheese
125 g/4 oz/½ cup natural fromage frais
125 g/4 oz blue cheese, cut into cubes
1 celery stalk, chopped finely
2 tsp snipped fresh chives
celery salt and pepper

MUSHROOMS IN SPICY TOMATO SAUCE

30 g/1 oz/2 tbsp butter or margarine
250 g/8 oz button mushrooms
150 g/5 oz/⅔ cup natural yogurt
1 tbsp tomato purée (paste)
2 tsp mild curry powder
salt and pepper

1 Scrub the potatoes and prick them with a fork. Bake in a preheated oven, 200°C/400°F/Gas Mark 6, for about 1 hour, until just tender.

2 To make the Mexican Sweetcorn Relish, put half the sweetcorn into a bowl. Put the remainder into a blender or food processor for 10–15 seconds, or chop and mash roughly by hand. Add the puréed sweetcorn to the sweetcorn kernels with the (bell) pepper, cucumber and chilli powder. Season to taste.

3 To make the Blue Cheese, Celery & Chive Filling, mix the soft cheese and fromage frais together until smooth. Add the blue cheese, celery and chives. Season with pepper and celery salt.

4 To make the Mushrooms in Spicy Tomato Sauce, melt the butter or margarine in a small frying pan (skillet). Add the mushrooms and cook gently for 3–4 minutes. Remove from the heat and stir in the yogurt, tomato purée (paste) and curry powder. Season to taste.

5 Wrap the cooked potatoes in foil and keep warm at the edge of the barbecue. Serve the fillings sprinkled with paprika or chilli powder or herbs.

Step *2*

Step *3*

Step *4*

Stuffed Red (Bell) Peppers

Stuffed (bell) peppers are a well-known dish, but this is a new version adapted for the barbecue.

SERVES 4

INGREDIENTS

2 red (bell) peppers,
halved lengthways and deseeded
2 tomatoes, halved
2 courgettes (zucchini),
sliced thinly lengthways
1 red onion, cut into 8 sections,
each section held together by the root
4 tbsp olive oil
2 tbsp fresh thyme leaves
60 g/2 oz/⅓ cup mixed basmati
and wild rice, cooked
salt and pepper

1 Put the (bell) peppers, tomatoes, courgettes (zucchini) and onion sections on to a baking sheet (cookie sheet). Brush the vegetables with olive oil and sprinkle over the thyme leaves.

2 Grill the (bell) pepper, onion and courgette (zucchini) over a medium barbecue for 6 minutes, turning once.

3 When the (bell) peppers are cooked, put a spoonful of the cooked rice into each one, with the onion and courgette (zucchini) on top.

4 Cook the tomato halves for 2–3 minutes only, before adding a half to each stuffed (bell) pepper. Season with plenty of salt and pepper and serve.

Step *1*

Step *2*

Step *3*

Roast Leeks

Use a good-quality French or Italian olive oil for this deliciously simple yet sophisticated vegetable accompaniment.

SERVES 4–6

INGREDIENTS

4 leeks
3 tbsp olive oil
2 tsp balsamic vinegar
sea salt and pepper

1 Halve the leeks lengthways, making sure that you hold the knife straight, so that the leek is held together by the root. Brush each leek liberally with the olive oil.

2 Cook over a hot barbecue for 6–7 minutes, turning once.

3 Remove the leeks from the barbecue and brush with the balsamic vinegar.

4 Sprinkle with salt and pepper and serve hot or warm.

 Step *1*

 Step *2*

Step *3*

Tofu (Bean Curd) & Mushroom Brochettes

These tofu (bean curd) and mushroom brochettes are marinated in a lemon,
garlic and herb mixture so that they soak up a delicious flavour.

SERVES 4

INGREDIENTS

1 lemon
1 garlic clove, crushed
4 tbsp olive oil
4 tbsp white wine vinegar
1 tbsp chopped fresh herbs, such as rosemary,
parsley and thyme
300 g/10 oz smoked tofu (bean curd)
350 g/12 oz cup mushrooms, wiped
salt and pepper
fresh herbs, to garnish

TO SERVE

mixed salad leaves (greens)
cherry tomatoes, halved

1 Grate the rind from the lemon finely and squeeze out the juice.

2 Add the garlic, olive oil, vinegar and herbs to the lemon rind and juice, mixing well. Season to taste.

3 Slice the tofu (bean curd) into large chunks. Thread the pieces on to metal or wooden skewers, alternating them with the mushrooms. If using wooden skewers, soak them in hand-hot water for 30 minutes.

4 Lay the kebabs in a shallow dish and pour over the marinade. Cover and chill for 1–2 hours, turning the kebabs in the marinade from time to time.

5 Cook the kebabs over the barbecue, brushing them with the marinade and turning often, for about 6 minutes.

6 Garnish with fresh herbs and serve with mixed salad leaves (greens) and cherry tomatoes.

Step *1*

Step *2*

Step *3*

Mozzarella with Barbecued Radicchio

*Sliced Mozzarella is served with tomatoes and radicchio, which is singed
over hot coals and drizzled with pesto dressing.*

SERVES 4

INGREDIENTS

500 g/1 lb Mozzarella
4 large tomatoes, sliced
2 radicchio

DRESSING

fresh basil leaves, to garnish
1 tbsp red or green pesto
6 tbsp virgin olive oil
3 tbsp red wine vinegar
handful of fresh basil leaves
salt and pepper

1 To make the dressing, mix the pesto, olive oil and red wine vinegar together.

2 Tear the fresh basil leaves into tiny pieces and add them to the dressing. Season with salt and pepper.

3 Slice the Mozzarella thinly and arrange it on 4 serving plates with the tomatoes.

4 Leaving the root end on the radicchio, slice each one into quarters. Barbecue them quickly, so that the leaves singe on the outside. Place two quarters on each serving plate.

5 Drizzle the dressing over the radicchio, cheese and tomatoes. Garnish with extra basil leaves and serve immediately.

Step *1*

Step *3*

Step *4*

DESSERTS

Vegetarian or not, confirmed pudding lovers feel a meal is lacking if there isn't a tempting dessert to finish off with. Desserts help satisfy a deep-seated desire for something sweet and they make us feel good. However, they are often loaded with fat and sugar which are notorious for piling on the calories.

The recipes in this chapter offer the ideal solution. They are light but full of flavour, so you can still enjoy that sweet treat without the bulging waistline and distended feeling at the end of a meal. This is particularly important after a vegetarian meal as the food can often be quite bulky and filling.

Most of the recipes are based on fruit, which is the perfect ingredient for healthy desserts that are every bit as tempting as those based on lavish amounts of cream and butter. Try the refreshing flavours of Green Fruit Salad with Mint & Lemon Syrup (page 248) or delicious Apricot Brûlée (page 238). We've also included one or two indulgences such as Boston Chocolate Pie (page 240) or Chocolate Chip Ice Cream (page 244).

Blackberry, Apple & Fresh Fig Compôte with Honey Yogurt

Elderflower cordial is used in the syrup for this refreshing fruit compôte, giving it a delightfully summery flavour.

SERVES 4

INGREDIENTS

1 lemon
60 g/2 oz/¼ cup caster (superfine) sugar
4 tbsp elderflower cordial
300 ml/½ pint/1¼ cups water
4 dessert (eating) apples
250 g/8 oz/2 cups blackberries
2 fresh figs

TOPPING

150 g/5 oz/⅔ cup thick natural yogurt
2 tbsp clear honey

1 Pare the rind from the lemon using a potato peeler. Squeeze the juice. Put the lemon rind and juice into a saucepan with the sugar, elderflower cordial and water. Heat gently and simmer, uncovered, for 10 minutes.

2 Peel, core and slice the apples, and add them to the saucepan. Simmer gently for about 4–5 minutes until just tender. Leave to cool.

3 Transfer the apples and syrup to a serving bowl and add the blackberries. Slice and add the figs. Stir gently to mix. Cover and chill until ready to serve.

4 Spoon the yogurt into a small serving bowl and drizzle the honey over the top. Cover and chill before serving.

Step *1*

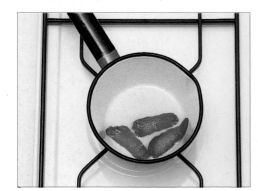

Step *2*

Step *3*

Apricot Brûlée

Serve this delicious dessert with crisp-baked meringues
for an extra-special occasion.

SERVES 6

INGREDIENTS

125 g/4 oz/²/₃ cup unsulphured dried apricots
150 ml/¹/₄ pint/²/₃ cup orange juice
4 egg yolks
2 tbsp caster sugar
150 ml/¹/₄ pint/²/₃ cup natural yogurt
150 ml/¹/₄ pint/²/₃ cup double (heavy) cream
1 tsp vanilla flavouring (extract)
90 g/3 oz/¹/₂ cup demerara sugar
meringues, to serve (optional)

1 Place the apricots and orange juice in a bowl and soak for at least 1 hour. Pour into a small pan, bring slowly to the boil and simmer for 20 minutes. Purée in a blender or food processor, or chop very finely and push through a sieve (strainer).

2 Beat together the egg yolks and sugar until the mixture is light and fluffy. Place the yogurt in a small pan, add the cream and vanilla and bring to the boil over a low heat.

3 Pour the yogurt mixture over the eggs, beating all the time, then transfer to the top of a double boiler, or place the bowl over a pan of simmering water. Stir until the custard thickens.

4 Divide the apricot mixture between 6 ramekins and carefully pour on the custard. Cool, then leave in the refrigerator to chill.

5 Heat the grill (broiler) to high. Sprinkle the demerara sugar evenly over the custard and grill (broil) until the sugar caramelizes. Set aside to cool. To serve the brûlée, crack the hard caramel topping with the back of a tablespoon.

 Step *3*

 Step *4*

Step *5*

Boston Chocolate Pie

This lighter version of the popular chocolate cream pie is made with yogurt and crème fraîche.

SERVES 6

INGREDIENTS

250 g/8 oz shortcrust pastry

CHOCOLATE CARAQUE

250 g/8 oz plain chocolate

FILLING

3 eggs
125 g/4 oz/½ cup caster sugar
60 g/2 oz/½ cup flour, plus extra for dusting
1 tbsp icing (confectioners') sugar
pinch of salt
1 tsp vanilla flavouring (extract)
400 ml/14 fl oz/1¾ cups milk
150 ml/¼ pint/⅔ cup natural yogurt
150 g/5 oz plain chocolate, broken into pieces
2 tbsp kirsch

TOPPING

150 ml/¼ pint/⅔ cup crème fraîche
Chocolate Caraque

1 Roll out the pastry and use to line a 23 cm/9 inch loose-bottomed flan tin. Prick the base with a fork, line with baking parchment and fill with dried beans. Bake blind in the preheated oven, 200°C/400°F/Gas 6, for 20 minutes. Remove the beans and paper and return to the oven for 5 minutes. Remove from the oven and leave on a wire rack to cool.

2 To make the Chocolate Caraque, spread pieces of chocolate on a large plate over a pan of simmering water until melted. Spread on to a cool surface with a palate knife. When cool, scrape it into curls by drawing a sharp knife firmly across the surface.

3 To make the filling, beat the eggs and sugar until light and fluffy. Put the flour, icing (confectioners') sugar and salt in a sieve, sift over the beaten eggs and stir until thoroughly blended. Stir in the vanilla flavouring.

4 Put the milk and yogurt in a small pan, bring slowly to the boil, then strain on to the egg mixture. Pour into the top of a double boiler, or a bowl over a pan of simmering water, and stir until thick enough to coat the back of a spoon.

5 Put the chocolate and kirsch into a small pan over a low heat. When it has melted, stir into the custard. Remove from the heat and stand the double boiler or bowl in cold water to prevent further cooking. Let cool .

6 Pour the chocolate mixture into the pastry case. Spread the crème fraîche over the chocolate, and arrange the caraque rolls on top.

Step *2*

Step *4*

Step *6*

Warm Currants in Cassis

*Crème de cassis is a blackcurrant–based liqueur which comes from
France and is an excellent flavouring for fruit dishes.*

SERVES 4

INGREDIENTS

375 g/12 oz blackcurrants
250 g/8 oz redcurrants
4 tbsp caster (superfine) sugar
grated rind and juice of 1 orange
2 tsp arrowroot
2 tbsp crème de cassis
whipped cream, to serve

1 Using a fork, strip the currants from their stalks and put in a saucepan.

2 Add the sugar and orange rind and juice, and heat gently until the sugar has dissolved. Bring to the boil and simmer gently for 5 minutes.

3 Strain the currants and place in a bowl then return the juice to the pan. Blend the arrowroot with a little water and mix into the juice then boil until thickened.

4 Leave to cool slightly, then stir in the cassis.

5 Serve in individual dishes with whipped cream.

Step *1*

Step *2*

Step *3*

Chocolate Chip Ice-Cream

This frozen dessert offers the best of both worlds, delicious cookies and a rich dairy-flavoured ice.

SERVES 6

INGREDIENTS

300 ml/½ pint/1¼ cups milk
1 vanilla pod
2 eggs
2 egg yolks
60 g/2 oz/¼ cup caster sugar
300 ml/½ pint/1¼ cups natural yogurt
125 g/4 oz chocolate chip cookies,
broken into small pieces

1 Pour the milk into a small pan, add the vanilla pod and bring slowly to the boil. Remove from the heat, cover the pan and leave to cool.

2 Beat the eggs and egg yolks in a double boiler, or in a bowl over a pan of simmering water. Add the sugar and continue beating until the mixture is pale and creamy.

3 Reheat the milk to simmering point and strain it over the egg mixture. Stir continuously until the custard is thick enough to coat the back of a spoon. Remove the custard from the heat and stand the pan or bowl in cold water to prevent any further cooking. Wash and dry the vanilla pod for future use.

4 Stir the yogurt into the cooled custard and beat until it is well blended. When the mixture is thoroughly cold, stir in the broken cookies.

5 Transfer the mixture to a chilled metal cake tin or polythene container, cover and freeze for 4 hours. Remove from the freezer every hour, transfer to a chilled bowl and beat vigorously to prevent ice crystals forming. Alternatively, freeze the mixture in an ice-cream maker, following the manufacturer's instructions.

6 To serve the ice-cream, transfer it to the main part of the refrigerator for 1 hour. Serve in scoops.

Step *1*

Step *4*

Step *5*

Cherry Clafoutis

*This is a hot dessert that is simple and quick to put together. Try the batter
with other fruits. Apricots and plums are particularly delicious.*

SERVES 6

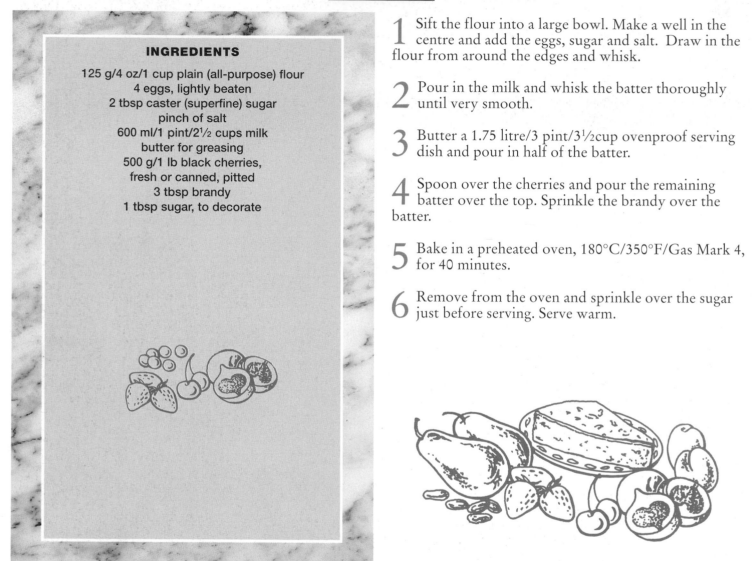

INGREDIENTS

125 g/4 oz/1 cup plain (all-purpose) flour
4 eggs, lightly beaten
2 tbsp caster (superfine) sugar
pinch of salt
600 ml/1 pint/2½ cups milk
butter for greasing
500 g/1 lb black cherries,
fresh or canned, pitted
3 tbsp brandy
1 tbsp sugar, to decorate

1 Sift the flour into a large bowl. Make a well in the centre and add the eggs, sugar and salt. Draw in the flour from around the edges and whisk.

2 Pour in the milk and whisk the batter thoroughly until very smooth.

3 Butter a 1.75 litre/3 pint/3½cup ovenproof serving dish and pour in half of the batter.

4 Spoon over the cherries and pour the remaining batter over the top. Sprinkle the brandy over the batter.

5 Bake in a preheated oven, 180°C/350°F/Gas Mark 4, for 40 minutes.

6 Remove from the oven and sprinkle over the sugar just before serving. Serve warm.

Step *1*

Step *2*

Step *4*

Green Fruit Salad with Mint & Lemon Syrup

This delightful fresh fruit salad is the perfect finale for a summer barbecue.
It has a lovely light syrup made with fresh mint and honey.

SERVES 4

INGREDIENTS

1 small Charentais or honeydew melon
2 green apples
2 kiwi fruit
125 g/4 oz/1 cup seedless white grapes
fresh mint sprigs, to decorate

SYRUP

1 lemon
150 ml/¼ pint/⅔ cup white wine
150 ml/¼ pint/⅔ cup water
4 tbsp clear honey
few sprigs of fresh mint

1 To make the syrup, pare the rind from the lemon using a potato peeler.

2 Put the lemon rind in a saucepan with the wine, water and honey. Bring to the boil, then simmer gently for 10 minutes. Remove from the heat. Add the sprigs of mint and leave to cool.

3 Slice the melon in half and scoop out the seeds. Use a melon baller or a teaspoon to make melon balls.

4 Core and chop the apples. Peel and slice the kiwi fruit.

5 Strain the cooled syrup into a serving bowl, removing and reserving the lemon rind and discarding the mint sprigs. Add the apple, grapes, kiwi and melon. Stir through gently to mix.

6 Serve, decorated with sprigs of fresh mint and some of the reserved lemon rind.

 Step *1*

 Step *3*

Step *5*

Passion Cake

Decorating this moist, rich carrot cake with sugared flowers lifts it into the celebration class. It is a perfect choice for Easter.

SERVES 8-10

INGREDIENTS

150 ml/¼ pint/⅔ cup corn oil
175 g/6 oz/¾ cup golden caster (superfine) sugar
4 tbsp natural yogurt
3 eggs, plus 1 extra yolk
1 tsp vanilla flavouring (extract)
125 g/4 oz/1 cup walnut pieces, chopped
175 g/6 oz carrots, grated
1 banana, mashed
175 g/ 6 oz/1½ cups plain (all-purpose) flour
90 g/3 oz/½ cup fine oatmeal
1 tsp bicarbonate of soda (baking soda)
1 tsp baking powder
1 tsp ground cinnamon
½ tsp salt

FROSTING

150 g/5 oz/generous ½ cup low-fat soft cheese
4 tbsp natural yogurt
90 g/3 oz/¾ cup icing (confectioners') sugar
1 tsp grated lemon rind
2 tsp lemon juice

DECORATION

primroses and violets
1 egg white, lightly beaten
45 g/1½ oz/3 tbsp caster (superfine) sugar

1 Grease and line a 23 cm/9 inch round cake tin (pan). Beat together the oil, sugar, yogurt, eggs, egg yolk and vanilla flavouring. Beat in the chopped walnuts, grated carrot and banana.

2 Sift together the remaining ingredients and gradually beat into the mixture.

3 Pour the mixture into the tin (pan) and level the surface. Bake in a preheated oven, 160°C/350°F/Gas Mark 4, for 1½ hours, or until firm. To test, insert a fine skewer into the centre: it should come out clean. Leave to cool in the tin (pan) for 15 minutes, then turn out on to a wire rack.

4 To make the frosting, beat together the cheese and yogurt. Sift in the icing (confectioner's) sugar and stir in the lemon rind and juice. Spread over the top and sides of the cake.

5 To prepare the decoration, dip the flowers quickly in the beaten egg white, then sprinkle with caster sugar to cover the surface completely. Place well apart on baking parchment. Leave in a warm, dry place for several hours until they are dry and crisp. Arrange the flowers in a pattern on top of the cake.

Step *3*

Step *4*

Step *5*

Cinnamon Pears with Maple & Ricotta Cream

These spicy sweet pears are accompanied by a delicious melt-in-the-mouth cream, which is relatively low in fat.

SERVES 4

INGREDIENTS

1 lemon
4 firm ripe pears
300 ml/½ pint/1¼ cups dry cider
or unsweetened apple juice
1 cinnamon stick, broken in half
mint leaves, to decorate

MAPLE RICOTTA CREAM

125 g/4 oz/½ cup medium-fat Ricotta
125 g/4 oz/½ cup low-fat natural fromage frais
½ tsp ground cinnamon
½ tsp grated lemon rind
1 tbsp maple syrup
lemon rind, to decorate

1 Using a vegetable peeler, remove the rind from the lemon and put in a non-stick frying pan (skillet). Squeeze the lemon and pour the juice into a shallow bowl.

2 Peel the pears, and halve and core them. Toss them in the lemon juice to prevent discolouration. Put in the frying pan (skillet) and pour over the lemon juice remaining in the bowl.

3 Add the cider or apple juice and the cinnamon stick. Gently bring to the boil, then lower the heat and simmer for 10 minutes. Remove the pears using a perforated spoon, reserving the cooking juice. Put the pears in a warm heatproof serving dish, cover with foil and keep warm in a low oven.

4 Return the pan to the heat, bring to the boil, then simmer for 8–10 minutes until reduced by half. Spoon over the pears.

5 To make the maple Ricotta cream, mix together all the ingredients. Decorate with lemon rind and serve with the pears.

Step *2*

Step *3*

Step *5*

INDEX